Stars Over England

Marc H. Penfield, MAFA

Material on the British monarchs first appeared in *ASPECTS*, the quarterly journal for Aquarius Workshops, Inc.

ISBN: 0-86690-453-0

First Printing: 1996
Current Printng: 2005

Cover Design: Jack Cipolla

Published by:
American Federation of Astrologers, Inc.
6535 S. Rural Road
Tempe, AZ 85285-2040

Printed in the United States of America

Dedication

Dedicated to
Elsie Landry, Moon in Leo
Bonnie Parker, Sun in Leo
and
Peggy Lance, Sun in Aquarius
whose friendship and support
over the years has meant a
great deal to me.

Contents

Part I
The Horoscope of England
and Its Progressions

The Natal Horoscope

England is the second oldest remaining monarchy on earth, after Japan. This island nation has been a model for other nations which have both a dynastic leader as well as an elected body of representatives. It was the world's first constitutional monarchy which elevated Parliament above the king or queen. The history of England has been one of war and conquest, shown by Aries rising, but also one of unified purpose and strong national pride illustrated by the Sun at the Midheaven in the sign of Capricorn.

When reading a mundane, or geopolitical, horoscope for the first time, a few differences must be taken into consideration. First, one must begin to think in pluralities as you're dealing not just with one individual but with thousands or millions of people. The delineation thus becomes somewhat impersonal and the words "you" and "they" take precedence over the singular "you," "he" or "she." It's like addressing an audience where one cannot see the individuals out there in the dark. A mundane chart outlines only the generalities, not specifics, or a nation when pertaining to its national identity or purpose.

Because of the size of the entity, the mundane chart is much more fated than is a natal horoscope. One could say that destiny plays a larger role than does free will. Transits and progressions in a mundane chart are reasonably clear cut and have little room for

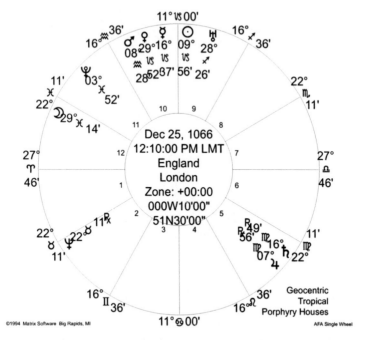

11° ♑ 00'

16° ♒ 36'

♂ 08° ♒ 52' ♀ 29°16' ♑ ☿ 09° ♑ 37' 56' ☉ 28° 26' ♅ 28° ♐

16° ♐ 36'

11' ♓ 22° ♇ 03° ♓ 52'

22° ♏ 11'

☽ 29° ♓ 14'

10   9

11

Dec 25, 1066
12:10:00 PM LMT
England
London
Zone: +00:00
000W10'00"
51N30'00"

8

27° ♈ 46'

12

7

27° ♎ 46'

1

6

22° ♉ 11' ♆ 22° ♉ 11° ♈ ℞

2

5

3   4

℞ 56' ♏ 49' ♃ 07° ♏ 16° ♄ 22° ♍

11' ♍

22° ♉ 11'

16° ♊ 36'

16° ♌ 36'

Geocentric
Tropical
Porphyry Houses

11° ♋ 00'

©1994 Matrix Software Big Rapids, MI

AFA Single Wheel

variables. If an aspect indicates that a particular event or situation is about to occur, then more often than not, it will happen. It's akin to what I term the "Titanic syndrome," whereby the size of an object determines its ability to thwart disaster or to propel itself forward into greener pastures. A rowboat, like an individual, can obviously see danger ahead and can take swift measures to ensure its safety. A larger entity like the Titanic or any large group of persons, for reasons outlined in physics, cannot so easily alter its course to avoid collision with an obstacle which might be inimical to its survival. When one deal with a mundane chart, one has to consider that free will is nonexistent. Political entities don't work that way despite what some very democratically inclined individuals would like to believe.

The age of an entity also bears consideration, for the older a nation or city is, the more likely it is to manifest the traits and characteristics shown in its horoscope. Nations like England, for example, have been around for generations and thus have had time to make an imprint signifying its uniqueness and individuality, even if it is

4

only in generalized terms. Newer nations, like Belgium or Yugoslavia, have been in existence for only a few generations os their "personalities" or "dispositions" are not as precise or distinctive. In a few countries like France and Italy, a combination of traits exists from former horoscopes drawn up centuries ago as well as from those republics which have been established in more recent times. In England, despite its being a constitutional monarchy, there is no dichotomy.

The meanings of the planets and the houses vary slightly from a natal chart to the mundane. The Sun in a natal chart signifies the individual will, inherent strength and purpose in life. In a mundane chart, it means all of the foregoing, but in plural terms, but the Sun mainly signifies the chief ruler, or monarch, or any nation or enterprise. The second house in a natal chart governs one's resources and assets—it's the same in a mundane chart but one must think in terms of national finances and banking activities. When one develops the ability to read a natal chart, reading the mundane horoscope should become relatively simple and straightforward, as there is little latitude for misinterpretation due to its rather fated nature.

I've chosen the chart of England to illustrate how mundane astrology works because its birth time is relatively undisputed. Coronations usually take place at high noon, thus the Sun and Midheaven will be reasonably close and more often than not, in the same degree and minute. I use the solar arc method to progress the Midheaven, rather than sidereal time as do some astrologers; thus, progressing one moves the other at the same rate of speed. I've chosen more than forty events in England's history which have been instrumental in its development as a nation.

Prior to William the Conqueror, England was hardly what one could call a unified country. Parts of Britain were ruled by local chieftains, some by Saxon kings and the Danes held sway over a large part along the North Sea. At the beginning of 1066, Edward the Confessor died, having on this deathbed willed the throne to Harold. He conveniently forgot that he had promised his kingdom to William of Normandy, his cousin, more than a decade earlier. When William heard that his inheritance, if not birthright, had been usurped by Harold, William took step to capture the throne for himself. After months of preparation, William left Normandy at the end of September, crossed the Channel and two weeks later fought Harold on the battlefield at Hastings. Harold was slain, thus making William the undisputed ruler of England. On Christmas, he was crowned in Westminster Abbey as William I. It was the last time this island was ever successfully invaded.

Looking at the chart for his coronation, we find four cardinal angles, five planets in mutable or common signs, and five planets in earth signs. This indicates that England is an active country which will impose its will on others, seldom taking a back seat or feeling sorry for itself. England will take charge and set the pace for others to follow due to those four angles in cardinal signs. The mutable planets signify that England is rather flexible, inclined to be more cerebral than would at first be supposed. An interest in literature, science and philosophy are indicated as well. The grouping in earth signs points to the English love of order and system, not to mention ambition for material goods.

The planets in Capricorn and the Midheaven typify the English. Having a stiff upper lip, they shall endure and prevail where other nations would falter or surrender. Ambitious, industrious and seeking to be the best, if not first in its field, England's desire to be "top banana" made it the base for the largest and most far-flung empire the world has ever known. Capricorn is one of the stronger signs of the zodiac and shines under adversity, seldom shirking its duty or relinquishing responsibility. Capricorn is also quite conscious of hierarchies and individual rank, thus the clearly defined class system which pervades English life from birth to death.

Capricorn is also conservative, cautious and extremely economical. The English are known to be frugal and somewhat spartan and hand down from generation to generation objects Americans might throw away. Some of the other keywords for Capricorn are honor, which, if acknowledged by persons of rank, grant one certain privileges, such as a title. No nation on earth seems to have as many "sirs," "lords" or "ladies" as does England. The honors are numerous and handed out according to individual effort or merit in one's chosen field of endeavor. Dependability and resilience are two more keywords for Capricorn, two traits which showed themselves to the fullest during the darkest days of World War II.

Mercury in Capricorn

Mercury in Capricorn indicates the English are plain speakers, methodical and systematic in their perceptions and seldom given to flights of fancy or illusion. Extremely organized, almost to a fault, they've followed a course of action and behavior through the years which might be called rigid and unyielding. Persevering against almost overwhelming odds, they've adopted new-fangled concepts slowly; they seem to prefer those things which have stood the test of time. Capricorn thinks in terms of the future and tries to see the big picture, not in what brings them only momentary pleasure. Mercury in Capricorn also accounts for their dry and often sardonic sense of humor, not to mention their love of bawdy lyrics and stage shows which clearly portray the more earthy side of life. This position of Mercury also indicates the English speak plainly and don't often go off on tangents. They stick to the straight and narrow.

Venus in Capricorn

Venus in Capricorn indicates that most English people have problems expressing their emotions. They seldom show their feelings in public and are always aware of propriety and decorum. Etiquette is important as are pomp and ceremony. This position of Venus shows the English love of rituals and formal ceremony, such as the changing of the guard. The English are traditional and their affections are often considered protective, like that of parents to their offspring. They seem to have a paternalistic view of the world and thus have the reputation of often being snobbish or condescending. It's simply that Capricorn types always seek the very best and won't settle for anything less. Venus in this sign also indicates the English love of countryside, not to mention gardening. Most inhabitants of this island have green thumbs and the climate allows an abundance of flowers and tress to grow profusely.

Moon in Pisces

The Moon in Pisces indicates that underneath this stiff upper lip lies an extremely sentimental and imaginative people, but since the Moon is in the twelfth house, most of those romantic illusions remain buried in the subconscious. The English are basically a kind

7

and gentle people who desire nothing more than to be left alone, untroubled by foreign elements which could easily disturb their lifestyle. The Moon in Pisces also shows the English to be a people who do indeed believe in things unseen, like ghosts or other forces often unaccepted by residents of other nations. Haunted houses in England are plentiful and they don't try to rationalize or analyze them. This lunar positions points to an interest in matters often called occult. This Pisces Moon in the twelfth house might also indicate England being an island, isolated from the continent, shrouded in fog and mist for most of the year. Since the Moon rules women in general, the typical Englishwoman seems to have taken a back seat to males to whom they have deferred in the past. The sextile of the Moon to Venus points to the English as being polite and very interested in social causes.

Mars in Aquarius

Mars in Aquarius indicates an English desire for freedom and independence, whether from monarchial tyranny or intrusions by the church or foreign leaders A strong humanitarian bent runs through the English—they always tried to leave their colonies better off than before the regions were first colonized. Despite the strong class system, the English consider themselves to be democratic, if not egalitarian. This position of Mars also shows itself in numerous inventions which have surfaced since the start of the Industrial Revolution two centuries ago. Strongly scientific and experimental by nature, the English react in an impersonal manner when dynamic and revolutionary methods are introduced into their realm of comprehension. Mars in a sign co-ruled by Saturn indicates a rather cold and reserved physical drive, but when awakened, watch out! The English can be real tigers when aroused and their unpredictability can surprise even the most jaundiced.

Jupiter in Virgo

Jupiter in Virgo indicates what is known as the work ethic and the English capacity for hard work. Residents of this island shine in matters where attention to detail is needed. Over the centuries, the English developed numerous skills which caused them to be at the forefront of the industrialized nations. Virgo is continually seeking to better itself and make our earthly existence more enjoyable for future generations. This position in Virgo also points to the English love of animals, especially dogs and horse on whom much affection and attention are displayed. Some have said the English relate better to their pets than they do to each other and that may be true. But the English don't love just anyone, for they're a highly discriminating people. You had better measure up or you're going to be left out in the cold.

Saturn in Virgo

Saturn in Virgo points to the common sense and technical ability which had made England a major industrial force in former years. Scientific advances and research carried on in its laboratories caused such illnesses as smallpox to disappear. Saturn in the sign of work and order illustrates the apprenticeship which pervaded England long ago. More often than not, a young man entered the same field as his father and remained there until he retired or dropped dead from exhaustion. Saturn in this sign also points to severe problems in the workplace, such as child labor, poverty and unemployment, all of which have surface during this century to a great degree. Saturn in the sign of health could also point to one of the most prevalent and persistent ailments of the English—arthritis and the feeling of being continually cold. Few homes or office buildings had central heating until recently.

Uranus in Sagittarius

Uranus in Sagittarius indicates the English desire for enlightenment and what is felt to be their spiritual mission to rule the world. Highly exploratory and curious about our planet, the English knew no equal where matters relating to settlement or colonization of foreign countries were concerned. Their idealistic, democratic and utopian philosophy inspired people around the world to copy their method of government and jurisprudence. Uranus in the sign of religion also points to their refusal to bend to authority figures like the Pope. Henry II was the first monarch to openly question church leadership and Henry VIII brought it full circle when he permanently broke with the Catholic church and made himself head of the Anglican church. English people are not accustomed to having others govern them, politically or philosophically. They are the masters of their souls, pure and simple.

Neptune in Taurus

Neptune in Taurus indicates the English love of physical beauty, be it from things growing in the ground, animals on the farm, or art and music. They dearly love their emerald isle, so resplendent and pastoral. Everyone who lives in an urban area years for a country retreat where one can be a country squire for a while. Neptune also deal with trends and fashion, and since Taurus is an earth sign, the English dress practically to ward off the cold and damp environment. Neptune in this earthy sign also points to love of material possessions which the English hang onto through the years, passing them from one generation to another. Ideals to the English are only as good as the extent to which they can be made practical in the long run; thus, they build for the future, which might explain why homes that would have been declared uninhabitable in other countries have lasted for centuries. This position of Neptune indicates the stubbornness and determinations, the "never say die" spirit for which the English are known. Their resilience and pugnacity is legendary, just like John Bull, their national symbol.

Pluto in Pisces

Pluto in Pisces indicates the universality and compassion of the English, especially in times of crisis. Highly impressionable and imaginative, the English are really much softer than the stiff picture they present to outsiders. They revel in tales of medieval knights and ladies and secretly long to return to the age of chivalry. Pluto in Pisces also indicates an ability for sacrifice in times of war and turmoil, and willingness on being led to the slaughter for national glory to preserve their unique lifestyle. Their subtle understanding of forces they cannot see or comprehend has sometimes led them to sit down and resign themselves to matters they cannot control. Progress in social situations comes slowly and England remains a land where tradition still holds sway over the more modern nations where industrialization has created societies prone to self-love, greed and materialism, often avoiding the ultimate spiritual mission of their country. England is in this respect a united country, one for all and all for one. Playing the game by the rules is more important than winning, for in the final analysis the chief satisfaction comes from being part of the whole, not isolated and separated from one's countrymen.

Aries Ascendant

Aries rising indicates a nation which has great capacity for leadership. Highly individualistic and seeking independence, the English have a reputation for being people who thrive on conflict and they have never been afraid to fight for what they believe. Rebellious and often crusading, the British enter foreign conflicts with banners flying and drums rolling and they've usually come out the victor. Impulsive and always assertive, they love sporting events, either as participants or as spectators. sometimes their enthusiasm gets out of control and they create conflict with authorities, as they did in Belgium a few years back. Aries always wants to be first and when combined with the desire for excellence (shown by the Sun in Capricorn), they give the appearance of egotists who think they know what's best for the rest of humanity. Impatient, they want it now, not tomorrow, which often gives them the ambition to rise above adversity.

The Aries Ascendant created an empire on which the Sun never set, but instilled in the hearts and minds of those they conquered the idea of autonomy and independence. The trine of Uranus to the Ascendant is well-shown in the preamble of the American Declaration of Independence whereby "life, liberty and the pursuit of happiness" are inalienable rights of all individuals. Coincidentally that planet which governs rebellion and freedom was discovered by an Englishman in 1781, the same year the Americans won their freedom from the mother country. Venus square the Ascendant and ruler of the Descendant indicates the fighting spirit of the English, seldom afraid to go to war and assert their right of eminent domain. As ruler of the second house, Venus also points to the love of possessions which was amply shown in the numerous wars for foreign territory during the first centuries of England's history.

Aspects within the chart of England are relatively close, the Sun trines both Jupiter and Saturn in Virgo and sextiles Pluto in Pisces. The Moon sextiles Venus and squares Uranus. Mercury trines Sat-

11

urn and Jupiter opposes Pluto and inconjuncts Mars. Neptune makes a wide trine to Saturn and Venus. But after working with this chart for many years, many progressions and transits operating at the time of a major event simply did not show up in the chart until I discovered the 30° dial. Then everything seemed to fall into place and my analysis and interpretation of the chart became more precise and accurate.

England's Chart on the 30° Dial

	0	15	
	1	16	♀ ♄
	2	17	
	3	18	
♇	4	19	
	5	20	
	6	21	
♃	7	22	♆
♂	8	23	
☉	9	24	
	10	25	
MC	11	26	
	12	27	Asc
	13	28	♅
	14	29	☽ ♀

For those unfamiliar with the 30° dial, it's much like using the 90° degree dial made popular by cosmobiologists. The 90° dial, however, concentrates on what they term "hard aspects" (the fourth harmonic) and thus eliminates other aspects which they term "soft." The 30° dial considers all aspects to be important, even those which are not generally considered so, such as the fifteen, seventy-five, 105 and 165 degree aspects. The best way to view the 30° dial is to get out a sheet of paper and on the left side list numbers from zero to fourteen; on the right side, list numbers from fifteen to twenty-nine. Now look at which numbers are across from one another: Any planet in the seventh degree, for example, will be in aspect to any planet in the twenty-second degree of any sign.

Looking at the chart of England, note that three planets occupy the seventh to ninth degrees, two planets occupy the sixteenth degree and three planets occupy either the twenty-eighth or twenty-ninth degree. Let's take the seventh degree first. Note that Jupiter sits opposite Neptune, an aspect one would normally miss when delineating this horoscope, using only a one degree orb for the 30° dial, note that Mars in the eighth degree is also "opposite" Neptune. The Sun in the ninth degree, however, does not aspect

Neptune as it's too far out of orb. Thus, whenever a major progression or transit hits either the seventh or eighth degree, it is affected by the nature of Jupiter, Mars and Neptune. The same holds true for planets in the twenty-eighth and twenty-ninth degrees. Many times foreign conflict took place when progressions or transits occupied this sector of the zodiac, but many times they did not. More often than not, planets were in the thirteenth and fourteenth degrees, the "opposite pole" of Uranus, the Moon and Venus on the 30° dial.

The 30° dial brings the horoscope into miniature form, eliminating both houses and aspects. One is really looking at a chart through a microscope and not being sidetracked by whether conventional astrological texts state a particular aspect is benefic or malefic. You're looking at numbers, nothing more. For example, when King John signed the Magna Carta in 1215, the progressed Midheaven at 7 Gemini 35 was square Jupiter, the planet of law. The Midheaven was also trine Mars, but without using the 30° dial, one would miss the "subtle" influence of Neptune and could not have accounted for why King John later chose to ignore this famous document.

Delineating and progressing a horoscope depends on having an accurate birth time. As previously stated, the birth time for this chart is almost beyond question, having been used for centuries. But after progressing the chart of England over nine centuries using Local Mean Time (LMT), something was clearly amiss, for the angles were off by two degrees or more, or ten minutes of clock time. Either I had my facts wrong or my interpretation was way out in left field. Soon the dilemma was solved: in ancient times, clocks with moving parts were not as yet invented and watches with moving pars weren't invented until the sixteenth century. The most widely used methods of keeping time were the sundial or the water clock. Every chart erected for the coronation of William the Conqueror used LMT, a concept not firmly established until the beginning of the nineteenth century with the arrival of the railroad. As fixed time zones weren't established until very late in the last century, we can't use GMT either. What time basis does one thus use? Try Local Apparent Time (LAT), which is based on the position of the Sun. The variation between LMT and LAT on the day of William's coronation is three minutes, forty-seven seconds. At high noon, the

Sun should thus occupy the position of 9 Capricorn 56, the same as the Midheaven, if one is using LAT. If one uses LMT, however, the Midheaven becomes 8 Capricorn 42. The chart for England thus had to be rectified and the degree I've chosen, 11 Capricorn 00, equates the 12:06:11 p.m. LAT. I know it's often sacrosanct to accept things as they are in certain astrological circles, but my skeptical and investigative nature seldom accepts what others deem to be workable without first testing things out. Without my rectification, the events in English history which we know to have occurred at a specific time would have happened two years (or more) later if one insists on using the chart based on LMT.

I firmly believe that the most potent aspects in a progressed chart are those made from the natal planets to the progressed angles. Throughout my three decades in astrology, I've found that whenever an angle progresses to an aspect of a natal planet, the nature of that aspected planet imbues itself on that individual or entity over the period of a year or two. Aspects of progressed angles to progressed planets are of secondary importance, sometimes they work, sometimes they don't. sometimes when an historical event appears to begin later than what is indicated in the progressed chart, one might be wise to look further to see if some relatively unimportant occurrence a year or two earlier might not have acted as the trigger point. With all this in mind, let's look at the chart of England progressed over nine centuries to the present day.

Note: All charts in this chapter are progressed from the 1066 chart of England.

Historical Events

The Domesday Survey—December 1085

During the reign of William the Conqueror, attention was focused on subjugating native tribes hostile to the Norman invasion. With the progressed Ascendant moving through Taurus, it was a time of building castles and constructing forts. The moment the progressed Midheaven entered Aquarius, it was deemed imperative to take a survey of the realm, to count its people and determine the assets of each individual. The progressed Sun was sextile the natal Moon, ruler of the fourth house of property and was conjunct natal Venus, ruler of the second house of assets. The ease with which this survey was taken is shown by Venus conjunct Mars; thus the rulers of the natal Ascendant and Descendant (the conquerors and the conquered) were in harmony.

Transiting Uranus at 9 Pisces opposing natal Jupiter and Neptune at 7 Cancer made favorable aspects to natal Jupiter as well. Many owners of property today can trace their lineage and holdings to this survey. Transiting Pluto was crossing the natal Moon, a further indication of the permanence and transformative nature of this event.

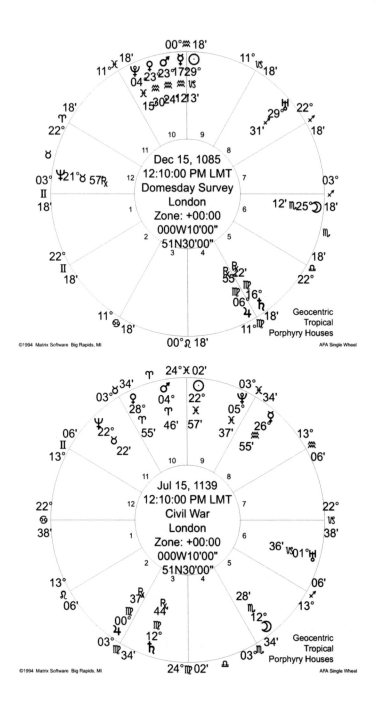

Chart 1:

00°≈18'

11°♓18'
Ψ 04° ♀23° ♂23° ☿17° ⊙29°
✕15°30'♒24'♑2'13'

11°♑18'

18°
♈22°

29°♐
31'31'
22°♐18'

♉03°
♇21°♉57℞
II 18'

Dec 15, 1085
12:10:00 PM LMT
Domesday Survey
London
Zone: +00:00
000W10'00"
51N30'00"

03°♐
12'♏25°☽18'

♏

II 22°
18'

55'℞22'
♍06°16° ♄18'
♃ 11°♍

18'
♎22°

11°
♋18'

00°♌18'

Geocentric
Tropical
Porphyry Houses

©1994 Matrix Software Big Rapids, MI

AFA Single Wheel

Chart 2:

24°♓02'

03°♉34'
♀28°♈ 55'
♂04°♈46'
⊙22°♓57'

03°♓34'
Ψ05°♓37'55'
☿26°♒

II 06'
22°♉22'

13°♒06'

22°
♋38'

Jul 15, 1139
12:10:00 PM LMT
Civil War
London
Zone: +00:00
000W10'00"
51N30'00"

22°♑38'

13°
♌06'

37'℞
♃00°♍
44'℞♄12'♍

28'♏12°☽

36'♑01°♅

03°♐13'

03°♍34'

03°♏34'

06'

24°♍02'

♎

Geocentric
Tropical
Porphyry Houses

©1994 Matrix Software Big Rapids, MI

AFA Single Wheel

16

Civil War—1139

On Henry I's death in 1135, the throne passed to Stephen, grandson of the Conqueror by his daughter, Adela, rather than to Henry's daughter, Matilda. The barons couldn't stomach the prospect of a woman occupying the throne. Matilda decided to fight for her inheritance, despite overwhelming odds, and in the summer of 1139 landed in England, thus precipitating a civil war which was to last for the next fourteen years. The progressed Midheaven at 24 Pisces semisquared natal Mars (ruler of war) and the progressed Ascendant at 22 Cancer opposed Mars and Jupiter on the 30° dial. The combination of these planets in later years brought dynastic or religious hostilities to the fore.

Three years before the Civil War began, transiting Uranus and Neptune opposed the natal Ascendant of England. When the war erupted, Uranus at 8 Scorpio was about to square natal Mars while Neptune at 0 Scorpio had just squared natal Venus. Pluto was sitting on top of Neptune. The war ended when the progressed Midheaven sextiled natal Mars.

The Murder of Becket—December 1170

When Henry II came to the throne, he centralized the government and, being dictatorial by nature, brooked no opposition from anyone, including the clergy. Shortly after Henry made Becket the Chancellor of England, he was appointed the Archbishop of Canterbury, as Henry felt his friendship with Becket would keep the church at bay. But Becket took his new position seriously and soon afterwards a conflict began between the crown and the church. Henry wished to be rid of Becket and some of his henchmen took him literally and slew Becket in the cathedral during vespers. One notes that the progressed Midheaven again negatively aspected the Sun and Mars on the 30° dial while the progressed Ascendant was sesquisquare natal Uranus in the ninth house of religion. Mars had progressed to the natal Ascendant, squaring natal Venus. It was a dark moment in Henry's reign and one which would severely test the loyalty of his subjects. Fortunately, progressed Saturn was trine the natal Sun.

Transiting Neptune was conjunct the Sun and Midheaven, caus-

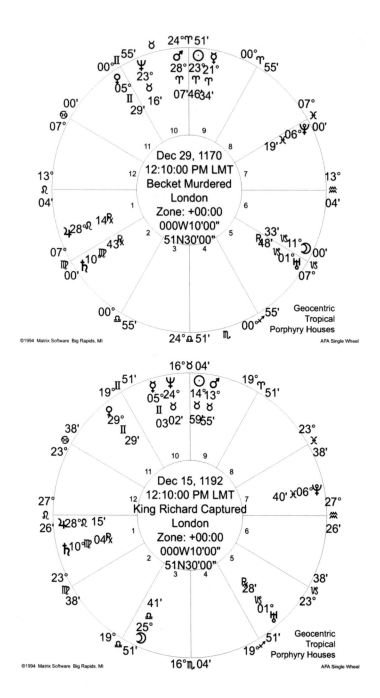

Geocentric
Tropical
Porphyry Houses

Dec 29, 1170
12:10:00 PM LMT
Becket Murdered
London
Zone: +00:00
000W10'00"
51N30'00"

©1994 Matrix Software Big Rapids, MI

AFA Single Wheel

Geocentric
Tropical
Porphyry Houses

Dec 15, 1192
12:10:00 PM LMT
King Richard Captured
London
Zone: +00:00
000W10'00"
51N30'00"

©1994 Matrix Software Big Rapids, MI

AFA Single Wheel

ing the scandal. Henry was forced to do penance to assuage the Church in Rome. The progressed Midheaven at 24 Aries would be prominent again during the time of Henry VIII when the religious issue surfaced again, this time causing the split to be permanent.

King Richard Captured—December 1192

During Richard's ten-year reign, he spent only a year in England. While returning home from a crusade in the Holy Land, Richard was captured and held for ransom by an Austrian vassal of the Holy Roman Emperor. The progressed Midheaven at 16 Taurus trined natal Mercury and Saturn while the progressed Ascendant trined natal Uranus in the ninth house and was conjunct progressed Jupiter, ruler of the natal ninth house. Venus, ruler of the natal seventh house of open enemies, opposed Uranus while Mars, ruler of the natal Ascendant, was sesquisquare Uranus. Because the progressed position of Jupiter and the Ascendant trined natal Uranus, Richard was set free a year and half later after his mother raised the ransom money. Transiting Pluto at 11 Cancer opposed the natal Midheaven, clearly illustrating the mob-like tactics involving extortion.

Magna Carta Signed—June 1215

Due to the personal and financial excesses during King John's reign, the barons decided it was time to put a halt to what they deemed was a threat to their superiority and privilege. On a meadow at Runnymede outside of London near Windsor, the king was cornered and forced to sign the Magna Carta (Great Charter), which has become one of the cornerstones of English government and the model for other nations seeking redress of grievances against tyranny or dictatorship. The progressed Midheaven at 7 Gemini squared natal Jupiter and Pluto, indicating a major power struggle. The Midheaven trine natal Mars (ruler of the Ascendant) at the same time the Sun was square progressed Pluto severely altered the role of the sovereign, forcing the head of state to relinquish prerogatives previously held by "divine right," thereby adjusting their rule to the whims of the barons. Progressed Mars at 29 Taurus 40 trined natal Venus, so war was avoided over this issue. Mars also sextiled the natal Moon, so by progression the ruler of the

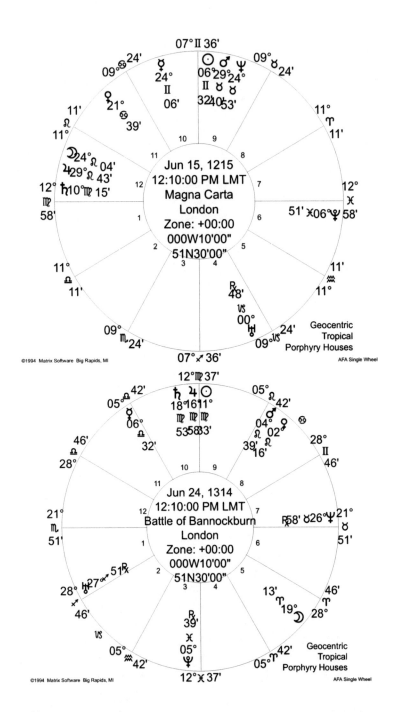

Jun 15, 1215
12:10:00 PM LMT
Magna Carta
London
Zone: +00:00
000W10'00"
51N30'00"

Geocentric
Tropical
Porphyry Houses

©1994 Matrix Software Big Rapids, MI

AFA Single Wheel

Jun 24, 1314
12:10:00 PM LMT
Battle of Bannockburn
London
Zone: +00:00
000W10'00"
51N30'00"

Geocentric
Tropical
Porphyry Houses

©1994 Matrix Software Big Rapids, MI

AFA Single Wheel

20

natal Ascendant, Descendant and IC came into harmony. But John tried to ignore the document as he considered himself above the law, shown by progressed Jupiter inconjunct the Moon and Venus. Progressed Saturn had retrograded back to a trine of the Sun, indicating the durability of this document which was amended in later years. Transiting Uranus at 0 Libra was trine natal Venus and opposing the Moon while transiting Pluto at 21 Leo squared Neptune.

Battle of Bannockburn—June 1314

Edward I conquered Wales in 1284 and Scotland a few years later. Under the reign of his son, Edward II, England lost Scotland to the forces of Robert the Bruce, whose superior military skill defeated the more numerous English troops. Thus did Scotland once again gain independence from Britain; it was formally recognized fourteen years later. The progressed Ascendant at 21 Scorpio opposed natal Neptune (ruler of the twelfth house of secrets and surprise), one of the most important planets in the English chart due to its aspects to Mars and Jupiter on the 30° dial. One might have thought England would have been victorious as progressed Jupiter was conjunct natal Saturn, but Saturn always places things on hold: Nearly four centuries later, Scotland and England were united under one crown and their union was made permanent. The sadness which gripped England over this defeat is well-shown by transiting Neptune at 25 Taurus, opposing the progressed Ascendant and semisquare the natal Midheaven. Transiting Pluto at 7 Pisces was opposing Jupiter, the planet of victory.

Hundred Years' War Begins—1337

On coming to the throne in 1327, Edward II claimed the throne of France from his mother's side. Ten years later, he made his bid known, thus precipitating the 100 Years' War—more like a series of battles and skirmishes than one long military assault. In 1337, England's progressed Midheaven at 5 Libra was inconjunct progressed Pluto while the progressed Ascendant at 6 Sagittarius was squaring that same planet. The first great land battle of this war took place at Crecy in 1346 when Jupiter and Saturn were trine natal Neptune. The Sun opposed Uranus on the 30° dial. Transiting Neptune at Crecy was conjunct Mars while Pluto at 11 Aries was squar-

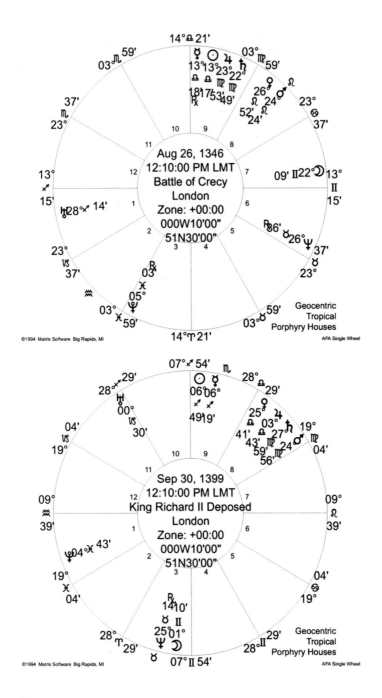

ing the natal Midheaven. Thus were the Midheaven and the rulers of the Ascendant and twelfth house in aspect at the first of many attempts to grab French territory.

Richard II Deposed—September 1399

Richard II was considered an ineffective monarch during his later years. Shortly after confiscating the estates of the powerful Lancaster family, a battle broke out with that branch of his family. The leader of the Lancasters, Henry Bolingbroke (later Henry IV) eventually prevailed, sending poor Richard to his doom. The progressed Midheaven at 7 Sagittarius squared natal Jupiter at the same time the progressed Ascendant had contacted natal Mars. By the time transiting Neptune opposed England's natal Ascendant, Richard II was murdered on the orders of the new king, the usurper known as Henry IV. One should also note the long lasting square of progressed Saturn to natal Uranus, an aspect which would be in force throughout most of the fifteenth century until the death of Richard III some 85 years later.

Battle of Agincourt—October 1415

Henry V vowed to renew the 100 Years' War which had languished for years. When the decisive battle at Agincourt, France took place, the progressed Midheaven was semisquare natal Mars while the progressed Ascendant at 14 Pisces 20 equalled the Moon, Venus, and Uranus on the 30° dial. Thus were the rulers of England's natal IC, Descendant, second and ninth houses aspected. Transiting Neptune at 10 Cancer opposed the natal Sun and Midheaven while Pluto at 22 Gemini aspected Mars, Jupiter, and Neptune on the 30° dial. This English victory would lay the groundwork for Henry V's son (Henry VI) to be crowned King of France in 1431, the same year Joan of Arc lost her life to the English overlords. The French finally ousted the English in 1453 as the progressed Ascendant squared natal Jupiter.

War of the Roses Begins—May 1455

Rivalries between the Houses of Lancaster and York had been simmering for years. As both dynasties were descended from Edward III, it was strictly a family squabble which led to the end of

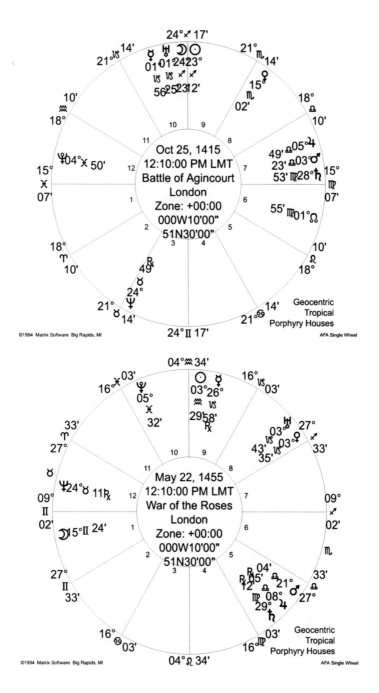

Oct 25, 1415
12:10:00 PM LMT
Battle of Agincourt
London
Zone: +00:00
000W10'00"
51N30'00"

Geocentric
Tropical
Porphyry Houses

©1994 Matrix Software Big Rapids, MI

AFA Single Wheel

May 22, 1455
12:10:00 PM LMT
War of the Roses
London
Zone: +00:00
000W10'00"
51N30'00"

Geocentric
Tropical
Porphyry Houses

©1994 Matrix Software Big Rapids, MI

AFA Single Wheel

feudalism and the Middle Ages in England. The war began on the field at St. Alban's as the progressed Ascendant trined natal Mars and progressed Jupiter and was inconjunct the natal Sun (kings). Jupiter had progressed to a trine of natal Mars while Saturn was trining natal Venus but opposing the Moon, indicating the family rivalry over the throne. Transiting Uranus at 8 Leo was opposing Mars, pointing to the violent and unpredictable nature of this war which in the end really benefitted no one. Edward IV took the throne from Henry VI who regained it briefly ten years later only to have his head cut off. After Edward's death, his brother, Richard III, usurped the throne for himself, placing the rightful heir, Edward V, in prison where he was probably murdered.

The Battle of Bosworth—August 1485

This battle ended the long warfare between the Houses of Lancaster and York, a truly Machiavellian period in English history which resulted in the usurper, Richard III, losing his life in battle to Henry Tudor, who then proceeded to vilify the vanquished. Henry Tudor agreed to marry Elizabeth York, daughter of Edward IV, thus

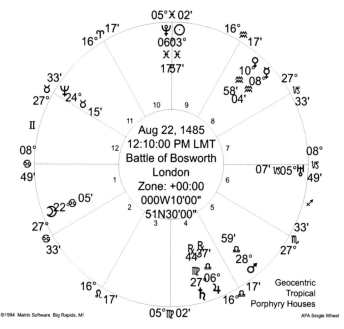

Aug 22, 1485
12:10:00 PM LMT
Battle of Bosworth
London
Zone: +00:00
000W10'00"
51N30'00"

Geocentric
Tropical
Porphyry Houses

©1994 Matrix Software Big Rapids, MI

AFA Single Wheel

uniting once and for all the warring branches of the family. The progressed Midheaven at 5 Pisces was about to conjunct progressed Pluto, indicating a rebirth and new beginning for the English monarchy. Direct descendants, called the Plantagenets, had ruled England since the days of Henry II, some three centuries before. Henry Tudor was a Welshman and only distantly related to former monarchs. The progressed Midheaven was also sextile progressed Uranus, indicating the quickness with which the new order took over. Progressed Mars at 28 Libra 59 had just completed its opposition to England's natal Ascendant but was sextiling natal Uranus, planet of freedom. The progressed Ascendant at 8 Cancer was sextile natal Jupiter as well. Progressed Saturn at 27 Virgo 44 indicated the major adjustment that had to be made with the monarchy to ensure its continuation as Saturn was inconjunct the natal Ascendant.

The Church of England—November 1534

As England followed the Salic Law which stated that no female shall rule in her own right, it was imperative that the monarch sire a male child to continue the succession. When Henry VIII's wife,

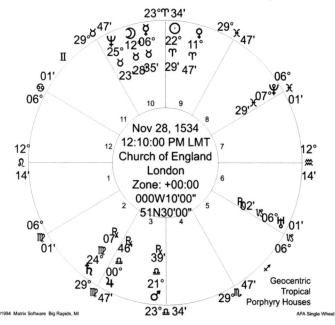

23°♈34'

Nov 28, 1534
12:10:00 PM LMT
Church of England
London
Zone: +00:00
000W10'00"
51N30'00"

Geocentric
Tropical
Porphyry Houses

©1994 Matrix Software Big Rapids, MI

AFA Single Wheel

23°♎34'

Catherine of Aragon, kept producing female offspring, Henry sought a divorce on the grounds he had married his brother's widow, which went against the Scriptures. Henry conveniently forgot that the Pope had already given a dispensation allowing Henry to marry Catherine and now Henry was asking the Pope to nullify his previous nullification.

As Henry sought solace in the arms of Anne Boleyn in 1528, England's progressed Midheaven at 17 Aries was still square natal Mercury: The progressed Ascendant opposed natal Mars. Henry married Anne in the spring of 1533, shortly before the birth of his daughter Elizabeth. During most of the following year, papers were drawn up making Henry VIII the head of the Church of England, also called the Anglican or Episcopal Church. The progressed Midheaven at 23 Aries 34 was semisquare progressed Pluto (power struggles) and sesquisquare natal Jupiter (religious issues). The progressed Sun was opposing progressed Mars, which was inconjunct natal Neptune about the time Henry started confiscating the monasteries and their property.

Henry got away with a lot of his antics due to Jupiter's progressed trine to Venus. Henry forced the populace to swear allegiance to his position as head of the church and those who refused were sent to their deaths. Transiting Uranus at 22 Cancer was sextiling natal Neptune while Neptune at 29 Pisces was crossing the Moon, indicating new religious and philosophical beliefs for the English. But Pluto was also squaring Uranus, so some hotbeds of resistance remained.

Drake Circumnavigates the World—December 1577

When Elizabeth ascended the throne, she made it state policy to thwart Spain on the high seas and gain a foothold in the New World. The progressed Ascendant was trine England's natal Midheaven, indicating future glory and fame for the crown. The progressed Midheaven was square natal Pluto when England took a stab at founding an empire in a part of the world which had already been carved up by Spain and Portugal. Progressed Jupiter at 28 Virgo was square natal Uranus, an aspect it would retain during Elizabeth's reign. Colonization wouldn't begin until Jupiter moved into the twenty-ninth degree, opposing England's natal Moon.

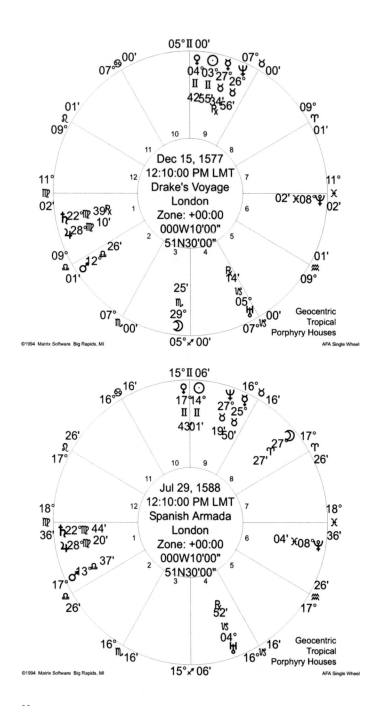

Chart 1 (top):

05° ♊ 00'

07° ♋ 00'

♀ ☉ ☿
04° 03° 27°
♊ ♊ ♉ Ψ
42'55'34' 26°
℞ 56'

07° ♉ 00'

01'
09° ♌

09° ♈ 01'

10   9

11
12   8

Dec 15, 1577
12:10:00 PM LMT
Drake's Voyage
London
Zone: +00:00
000W10'00"
51N30'00"

11° ♍ 02'

7

11° ♓ 02'

♄ 22° ♍ 39' ℞
♃ 28° ♍ 10'

1   6

02' ♓ 08' Ψ

2   5

09° ♎ 01'

♂ 12° ♎ 26'

3   4

01'
♒ 09°

07° ♏ 00'

25'
♏ 29'
☽

℞ 14'
♑ 05°
♅ 00'
07° ♑

Geocentric
Tropical
Porphyry Houses

05° ♐ 00'

©1994 Matrix Software Big Rapids, MI

AFA Single Wheel

Chart 2 (bottom):

15° ♊ 06'

16° ♋ 16'

♀ ☉
17° 14°
♊ ♊
43' 01'

Ψ ☿
27° 25°
♉ ♉
19° 50'

16° ♉ 16'

♈ 27' ☽ 27°
17° ♈ 26'

26'
17° ♌

10   9

11
12   8

Jul 29, 1588
12:10:00 PM LMT
Spanish Armada
London
Zone: +00:00
000W10'00"
51N30'00"

18° ♍ 36'

7

18° ♓ 36'

♄ 22° ♍ 44'
♃ 28° ♍ 20'

1   6

04' ♓ 08' Ψ

2   5

17° ♎ 26'

♂ 13° ♎ 37'

3   4

26'
♒ 17°

16° ♏ 16'

℞ 52'
♑ 04°
♅
16° ♑ 16'

Geocentric
Tropical
Porphyry Houses

15° ♐ 06'

©1994 Matrix Software Big Rapids, MI

AFA Single Wheel

28

Transiting Uranus at 8 Cancer opposed the Sun and sextiled Jupiter, indicating the risk and gamble England took at this venture. Transiting Pluto had just crossed the Moon (ruler of the IC) and was still within orb to a sextile of Venus (ruler of the Descendant and second house of assets).

The Spanish Armada—August 1588

For three decades, Philip II of Spain had tried to appease his former sister-in-law Elizabeth, but when Good Queen Bess executed Mary Queen of Scots, the stage was set to avenge the dead queen as Scotland was an ally of Spain. The largest armada ever assembled headed for the British Isles and England trembled at the thought of an invasion: They had neither the money to buy ships from their allies nor the ships to ward off an attack. The progressed Midheaven equalled the Moon and Venus on the 30° dial while the Ascendant equaled Pluto. However, the progressed Sun was trine progressed Mars and progressed Mars equalled the Moon and Uranus on the dial. Saturn was also trining natal Neptune, lord of the high seas and tempests. The odds were not in England's favor but at the last minute the weather turned nasty and the English were able to route the armada around the north of Scotland and across the Irish Sea. Victory meant that England's power on the high seas was assured and the establishment of an empire no longer a wistful dream. Transiting Uranus at 14 Pisces squared the progressed Midheaven, illustrating the sudden and fortunate turn of events for the English.

East India Company Established—December 1600

To manage the properties England was about to acquire in the Far East, Elizabeth founded an organization which was to last for two and a half centuries. Its supremacy in governmental affairs was eventually eliminated in India, but for generations the East India Company paved the way for conquest and empire building in Asia. The progressed Midheaven at 26 Gemini was about to oppose natal Uranus while the progressed Ascendant was square that same planet of exploration. Uranus rules the eleventh house in the English chart and occupies the ninth house, so national objectives have often been focused on foreign exploration. It might be wise at this time to note that Queen Elizabeth I's Ascendant was 28 Sagittarius

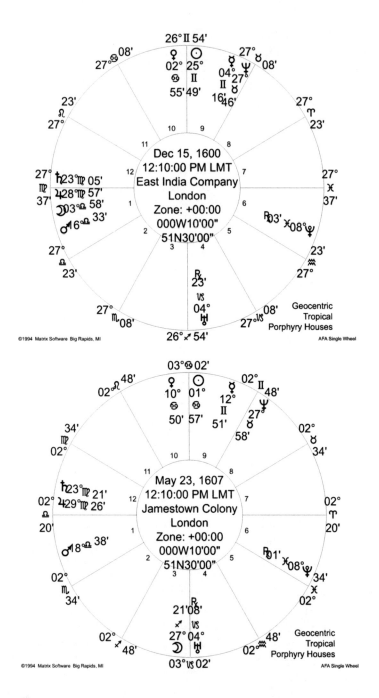

Chart 1 — East India Company

26° ♊ 54'

♀ 02° ♋ 55'
☉ 25° ♊ 49'

27° ♋ 08'

☿ 04° ♊ 16'
♃ 27° ♉
♄ 46'
♆ ♉ 08'

27° ♈ 23'

27° ♍ 37'
♄ 23° ♍ 05'
♃ 28° ♍ 57'
☽ 03° ♎ 58'
♂ 16° ♎ 33'

Dec 15, 1600
12:10:00 PM LMT
East India Company
London
Zone: +00:00
000W10'00"
51N30'00"

27° ♓ 37'

27° ♎ 23'

℞ 03' ♓ 08° ♇

27° ♏ 08'

23'
♒
27°

℞ 23'
♑ 04°
♅

26° ♐ 54'

Geocentric
Tropical
Porphyry Houses

©1994 Matrix Software Big Rapids, MI

AFA Single Wheel

Chart 2 — Jamestown Colony

03° ♋ 02'

♀ 10° ♋ 50'
☉ 01° ♋ 57'

☿ 12° ♊ 51'

02° ♊ 48'
♆ 27° ♉ 58'

02° ♑ 48'

02° ♍
34'

02° ♉ 34'

♄ 23° ♍ 21'
♃ 29° ♍ 26'

02° ♎
20'

May 23, 1607
12:10:00 PM LMT
Jamestown Colony
London
Zone: +00:00
000W10'00"
51N30'00"

02° ♈ 20'

♂ 18° ♎ 38'

02° ♏
34'

℞ 01' ♓ 08° ♇

02° ♓ 34'

02° ♐ 48'

℞ 21'
♐ ♑
27° 04'
☽ ♅

02° ♒ 48'

03° ♑ 02'

Geocentric
Tropical
Porphyry Houses

©1994 Matrix Software Big Rapids, MI

AFA Single Wheel

conjunct England's natal Uranus, thus explaining her obsession with foreign conquest during her long reign of forty-five years.

Jamestown Founded—May 1607

The first permanent English settlement in America was named after King James I, who made it national policy to continue where Elizabeth left off regarding colonization and exploration. Progressed Venus opposed the natal Sun and Midheaven while the progressed Midheaven was trine Pluto, indicative of a new direction and eventual transformation of English foreign policy. Progressed Jupiter had now moved out of orb to the square to natal Uranus and was now opposite the natal Moon (ruler of the IC) and about to trine natal Venus (ruler of the Descendant). Thus were the rulers of the fourth house (residence), second house (financial assets), seventh house (foreign alliances and partnerships) brought into play with the ruler of the ninth house of foreign interests. Transiting Uranus at 29 Taurus made favorable aspects to Venus and the Moon while Neptune at 11 Virgo was trine England's Sun and Midheaven. Pluto at 3 Taurus was sextile its own position as well as the progressed Midheaven at the time Jamestown was settled.

Thirteen years later, colonists originally heading for Jamestown were blown off course and landed in Plymouth, Massachusetts. Transiting Pluto at 11 Taurus was trine the natal Sun and Midheaven. These two colonies, the south (Neptune) and north (Pluto) were two distinct societies whose cultural rivalries would erupt into the American Civil War some 250 years later due to their basic ideological differences and economic disparities.

English Civil War Begins—August 1642

The Stuart kings believed in their divine right to rule, not just to reign. Charles I had dismissed Parliament in 1629 as transiting Uranus at 10 Virgo trined England's natal Sun and Midheaven. During the following decade, Charles laid the groundwork for the civil war which erupted shortly after he tried to have the leaders of the reconvened Parliament arrested. Charles took up the banner of the Royalists against Cromwell's troops, called the Roundheads. The conflict would last for six and a half years until Charles lost his head. When the civil war began, the progressed Midheaven was

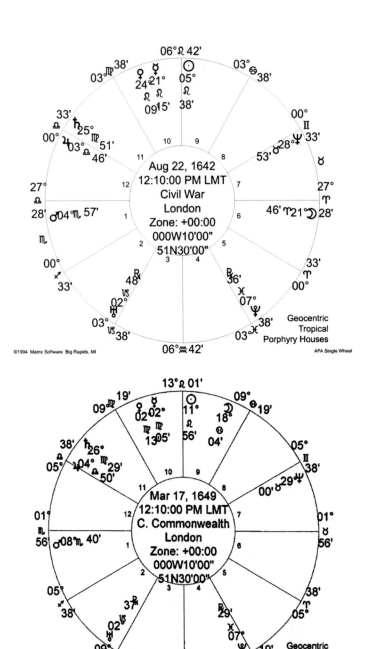

Aug 22, 1642
12:10:00 PM LMT
Civil War
London
Zone: +00:00
000W10'00"
51N30'00"

Geocentric
Tropical
Porphyry Houses

©1994 Matrix Software Big Rapids, MI

AFA Single Wheel

Mar 17, 1649
12:10:00 PM LMT
C. Commonwealth
London
Zone: +00:00
000W10'00"
51N30'00"

Geocentric
Tropical
Porphyry Houses

1994 Matrix Software Big Rapids, MI

AFA Single W

inconjunct progressed Pluto while the progressed Ascendant was sextile natal Uranus. It would be a thirst for freedom in the English desire to rid themselves of the dictatorial and tyrannical rule of Charles I. The progressed Sun was squaring progressed Mars while Mercury squared natal Neptune, the planet of idealism and often misguided causes.

Transiting Uranus at 8 Scorpio was square natal Mars, but the fortunate aspects to natal Jupiter and the Sun indicated the war would eventually produce a more democratic government. Transiting Neptune at 26 Scorpio was semisquare the natal Midheaven and Pluto had just squared its own position in early Gemini.

Commonwealth Founded—February 1649

With the execution of Charles I for high treason the month before, England became a republic of sorts with Oliver Cromwell as leader. During his nine-year rule, England became a dictatorship or virtual police state under the command of the military. The progressed Midheaven was sesquisquare natal Uranus, indicating the stress in attaining real freedom and democratic reform. The progressed Ascendant sextile progressed Mercury, Venus and Uranus demanded the English bend to the perverted whims of Uranian ideals; with Mars squaring its own position, the English had simply traded one tyrant for another. It was a time of austerity and severity, and frivolity was frowned upon. Times were drab: The Puritans had taken over. I've often found that whenever a strong Uranian aspect occurs, freedom flies out the window and a totalitarian viewpoint develops. By 1660, the Stuart line was restored as the progressed Ascendant at 9 Scorpio sextiled England's natal Sun. The progressed Midheaven at 24 Leo was in aspect to that same planet of joy, mirth and enjoyment. Neptune was crossing the natal Sun as the Restoration began under Charles II, a man temperamentally the opposite of Cromwell.

The Glorious Revolution—December 1688

With the death of Charles II in 1685, his brother James II ascended to the throne. James had converted to Catholicism some years earlier, which by itself posed no problem as there was no direct heir to the throne. However, when his wife gave birth to a son in

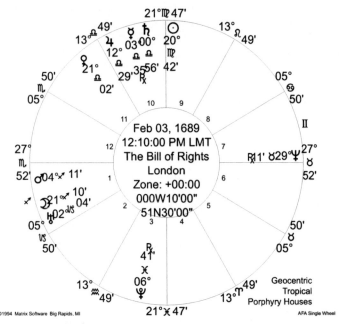

21°♏47'

13°♎49'   ☿ ♄   ☉
12°03°00° 20°
21°   ♎   ♎   ♏
♀   29°35°56' 42'
50'   02'   ℞
♏
05°   10   9

13°♌49'

05°
♋
50'

11   8   Ⅱ

27°   12   Feb 03, 1689   7   ℞11' ♉29°♆ 27°
♏   12:10:00 PM LMT   ♉
52'   ♂04°♐11'   1   The Bill of Rights   6   52'
London
♐ ♅21°♒10'   2   Zone: +00:00   5
♃02°♑04'   000W10'00"
05°   51N30'00"
♑   3   4   50'
50'   ♉
♌   05°
4♈℞

♓

06°   49'
♆   13°♈   Geocentric
13°♒49'   21°♓47'   Tropical
Porphyry Houses

©1994 Matrix Software Big Rapids, MI   AFA Single Wheel

June 1688, the British became apprehensive over a continued
Catholic succession and a revolution broke out five months later
which eventually sent James II into exile. Parliament then offered
the throne to his daughter Mary,who agreed to rule if she could do
so with the aid of her husband, William of Orange. The progressed Midheaven at 21 Virgo 47 was trine natal Neptune, one of
the planets involved whenever a religious dispute erupts in England. Progressed Saturn had just entered Libra, so the British
wanted a guarantee that their rights would not be denied them by
the crown. William and Mary agreed to the Bill of Rights in early
1689, just as transiting Neptune at 10 Pisces was sextiling England's natal Midheaven and Sun. During this turbulent period,
transiting Pluto was squaring the natal Ascendant, paving the path
for renewal of individual rights and usurpation of monarchial
privileges.

War of the Spanish Succession—May 1702

When the Spanish king died in 1701 without an heir, a dilemma
arose as to who would sit on the Spanish throne. Many claimants

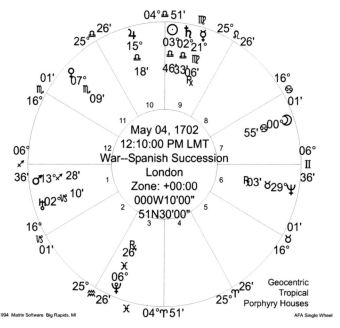

04°♎51' ♍

25°♎26' ♃15°
♎18'

☉ ♄ ☿
03°02°21'
♎ ♎ ♍
46°33°06'
℞

25°♌26'

01'
♀07°
♏
16° ♏09'

16°
♋
01'

10   9

06°
♐
36'   ♂13°♐28'   1

11   8

May 04, 1702
12:10:00 PM LMT
War--Spanish Succession
London
Zone: +00:00
000W10'00"
51N30'00"

7

06°
♊
36'

55'♋00°☽

♃02°♑10'

2   5

12

3   4

6   ℞03'♉29'♆

16°
♑
01'

01'
♉
16°

16°
♑
01'

℞26'♈

06°
♓
25° ♆
♏26'

26'♈
25°♈

Geocentric
Tropical
Porphyry Houses

©1994 Matrix Software Big Rapids, MI   ♓ 04°♈51'   AFA Single Wheel

came forth but none had clear title. Charles had left the throne to the grandson of Louis XIV of France, but as France was already the most powerful nation on the continent, Europeans trembled at the thought of one monarch ruling both countries. In essence, France would annex Spain. An alliance was formed between England, Holland, Prussia and Austria against the French.

England's progressed Ascendant was squaring progressed Pluto while the progressed Sun at 3 Libra was inconjunct natal Pluto. Over the next few years, England won many important battles on land and sea: Blenheim in 1704 and Gibraltar in 1705 were the most remembered. The threat to England's supremacy and security was shown by transiting Neptune at 11 Aries square the natal Midheaven. The war ended in 1713 when Spain and France agreed to remain separate nations. By then, the Midheaven had progressed to a conjunction of progressed Jupiter.

Union of England and Scotland—May 1707

The crowns of these two countries were united under James I in 1603, but each nation kept its own laws and Parliament. To correct

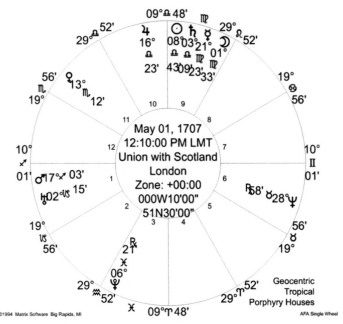

09°♎48' ♍

♃   ☉   ♄   ☿   29°
16°   08 03   21°   ☽   ♌52'
♎   ♎ ♎   ♍   01°
23'   43 09 23'   ♍
        33'

29°♎52'

56'   ♀13°
19°   ♏   ♏12'

19°
⊛
56'

10°
♐
01'   ♂17°♑03'
  ♅02°♑15'

10°
Ⅱ
01'

May 01, 1707
12:10:00 PM LMT
Union with Scotland
London
Zone: +00:00
000W10'00"
51N30'00"

℞58'   ♉28°♆

19°
♑
56'

21℞
♓
06°

52'
29°♈52'

56'
♉
19°

29°   ♆
♒52'   ♓   09°♈48'

Geocentric
Tropical
Porphyry Houses

©1994 Matrix Software Big Rapids, MI   AFA Single Wheel

this anomaly, an act was drawn up to eliminate most, but not all, of their individual political differences. The progressed Midheaven at 9 Libra was squaring England's natal Sun and the progressed Sun was trine natal Mars, ruler of the natal Ascendant. However, Mars was squaring natal Saturn, ruler of the governmental tenth house, so further rebellions would erupt between the English and the Jacobites (followers of Bonnie Prince Charlie) over the next four decades. Loss of freedom for the Scots was shown by transiting Uranus at 9 Leo opposing natal Mars, ruler of warfare.

England Wins Canada—September 1759

The closing years of George II's reign were glorious for England. It had conquered India in 1757 under the military genius of Robert Clive as the progressed Midheaven in late Scorpio sextiled natal Venus (ruler of the seventh house of war) and trined the natal Moon (ruler of the fourth house of territorial acquisition). With the defeat of the French on the Plains of Abraham in Quebec, the English gained considerable land in the New World. The progressed Ascendant had just entered Aquarius and was within orb to natal

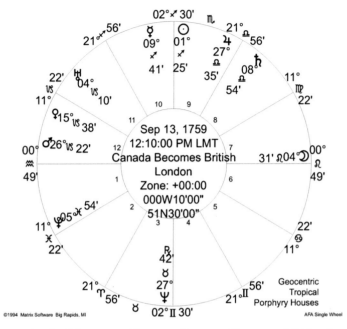

02°✗ 30' ♏

21°✗ 56'   ☿ ☉   21°♎
         09° 01°   56'
         ✗ ✗   24
         41' 25'   27°
                 ♎   ♄
22' ♅ 04°   35'   08°
♑ ♑   54'   11°
11°   10'   10   9   ♍ 22'

♀15°♑ 38'   11   8

00° ♂26°♑ 22'   12 Sep 13, 1759   7   31' ♌04°☽ 00°
♒   12:10:00 PM LMT   ♌
49'   1 Canada Becomes British 6   49'
                London
             ♇05°✗ 54' Zone: +00:00
11°   2 000W10'00" 5   22'
♓   51N30'00"   ♋
22'   3   4   11°

                 ℞
                 42'
21°   27°   56'   Geocentric
♈ 56'   ♆   21°♊   Tropical
             ♉ 02°♊ 30'   Porphyry Houses

©1994 Matrix Software Big Rapids, MI   AFA Single Wheel

Venus, lord of the second house of assets. Venus at 15 Capricorn was trine natal Saturn while Mars at 26 Capricorn was about to square the natal Ascendant. The joint victories in India and Canada are also shown by progressed Jupiter at 27 Libra 35 opposing the natal Ascendant (Jupiter governs the ninth house of foreign interests) as well as Saturn trine natal Mars. All of the above aspects added much prestige to the Crown.

Transiting Uranus at 29 Pisces was conjunct England's natal Moon and sextile Venus at the same time Uranus was squaring Uranus, ruler of the ninth house. With the addition of India and Canada, England now ruled more than six million square miles, the largest empire the world had ever known.

America Declares Its Independence—July 1776

When George III came to the throne, the American colonists fought against his restrictive policies such as the Stamp Act and the tax on tea. When the American Revolution began in 1775, England's progressed Ascendant had just entered Pisces. When the colonies declared their independence a year later, the progressed As-

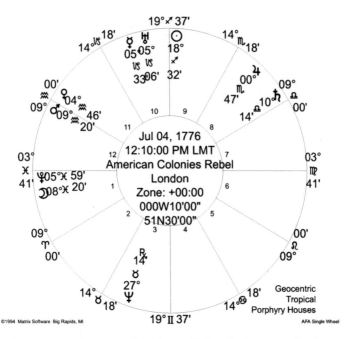

19°✗37'

14°♑18'   ☿ ♅   ☉
           05 05° 18°
           ♑ ♑   ✗
           33 06' 32'

14°♏18'

00'   00'♃
♒   ♏   09°
04°   47'   ♎
09°♒ ♂   14° 10°♄ 00'
     09°♒46'

03°   Jul 04, 1776   03°
♓   12:10:00 PM LMT   ♍
41' ♀05°♓59'   American Colonies Rebel 41'
     ☽8°♓20'   London
                 Zone: +00:00
                 000W10'00"
                 51N30'00"

09°   00'
♈   ♌
00'   09°

14°♉   R   18°   Geocentric
     18'   14✗   14°♋ Tropical
              ♉   Porphyry Houses
              27°
              ♆
©1994 Matrix Software Big Rapids, MI   19°♊37'   AFA Single Wheel

cendant was conjunct natal Pluto and Mars had returned to its natal position. Progressed Mercury was conjunct progressed Uranus at the same time Jupiter was squaring natal Venus—not a good omen for England winning the war with the colonists.

The loss of the colonies in October 1781 was a severe blow to England's dream of an empire in the New World. In 1776, transiting Uranus at 8 Gemini was trine natal Mars, Neptune at 22 Virgo was trine its natal position, but transiting Pluto at 27 Capricorn was square the natal Ascendant. As Pluto rules the eighth house, which has to do with debts and financial losses, the loss of revenue was a severe blow to English pride. In 1781, transiting Uranus at 10 Cancer opposed England's natal Sun and Midheaven, while Pluto, at 7 Aquarius in 1783 when the Treaty of Paris was signed, pointed to the irrevocability of friendship at arms.

Australia Settled—January 1788

Because the Americans had won their freedom, England had to find another site to house the convicts then crowding its gaols. The unexplored continent of Australia was chosen as the most suitable

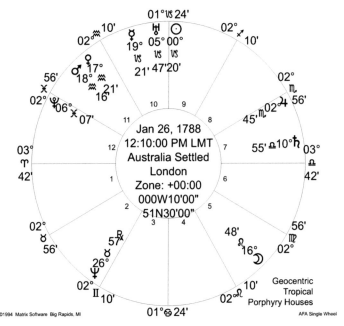

01°ɪ524'

02°♒10'   ☿ 19° ♅ 05° ⊙ 00°
                 ℣ ℣ ℣
56' ♂ 17° ♒   21' 47'20'
  ✶ 18° ♒
02° ♆ 16° 21'
    06° ✶   10   9
      07'   11   8   45' ♏ 02°♃56'
                Jan 26, 1788
03° 12   12:10:00 PM LMT 7   55' ♎10°♄03°
♈   Australia Settled   ♎
42'   1   London   6   42'
           Zone: +00:00
         000W10'00"
      2   51N30'00"   5
           3   4
02° ♉   48'   56'
56'   57° ♃   ♌16° ♍02° ♍
    26° ♉   ☽
    ♆
02°   10' Geocentric
  ♊10'   02°♌ Tropical
                      Porphyry Houses
©1994 Matrix Software Big Rapids, MI   01°♋24'   AFA Single Wheel

site as it was distant from the centers of world power. The first fleet of ships left Portsmouth in May 1787 and, after a journey of eight months, landed at Botany Bay near Sydney. The progressed Midheaven had just entered Capricorn and would shortly sextile progressed Jupiter, ruler of the ninth house. Transiting Uranus at 27 Cancer squared England's natal Ascendant and Neptune at 21 Libra was inconjunct its own position. Neptune rules prisons and convicts as well as long journeys over the ocean.

War with France—February 1793

Over the previous seven centuries, England had fought its neighbor France so many times that another conflict seemed unlikely to provoke much interest. The French Revolution had begun in July 1789, but four years later the Reign of Terror under Robespierre caused considerable alarm in certain circles about the political security of Europe. The progressed Midheaven at 6 Capricorn trined natal Jupiter, indicating that England would eventually triumph over the French. Venus and Mars both squared natal Neptune, indicating that naval activity would highlight this war (Gibraltar and

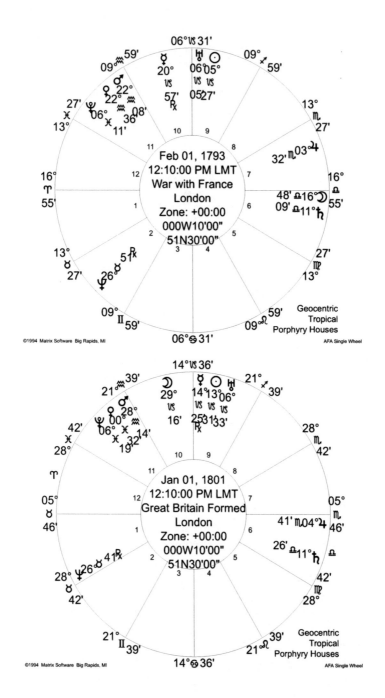

Feb 01, 1793
12:10:00 PM LMT
War with France
London
Zone: +00:00
000W10'00"
51N30'00"

Geocentric
Tropical
Porphyry Houses

©1994 Matrix Software Big Rapids, MI

AFA Single Wheel

Jan 01, 1801
12:10:00 PM LMT
Great Britain Formed
London
Zone: +00:00
000W10'00"
51N30'00"

Geocentric
Tropical
Porphyry Houses

©1994 Matrix Software Big Rapids, MI

AFA Single Wheel

Trafalgar). Transiting Uranus at 22 Leo and transiting Pluto at 22 Aquarius also squared England's natal Neptune.

Great Britain Established—January 1801

Henry II had conquered Ireland in the late twelfth century, but attempts by the English to govern this troubled and rebellious island came to naught over the following six centuries. To assuage the Irish, some form of political representation was promulgated in the English Parliament: The Union of Great Britain, Scotland and Ireland was born. The progressed Midheaven was conjunct progressed Mercury (ruler of the third house of neighboring countries) but the progressed Ascendant at 5 Taurus opposite progressed Jupiter (ruler of the ninth house) was indicative of further Irish resistance against their English masters. Mars sextiled the natal Ascendant and Uranus, indicating eventual freedom for the Irish.

Transiting Uranus at 0 Libra opposed the Moon but trined Venus, a catch-22 situation demanding diplomacy and compromise if the union were to last. The Irish were against this act from the beginning: It took them another 120 years to gain their complete freedom.

War with the USA—June 1812

In the midst of fighting the French under Napoleon, another conflict erupted over England's impressment (kidnapping) of American sailors to man their own vessels. The Americans finally had enough and declared war, thus splitting English forces on two fronts. The progressed Midheaven was about to square England's natal Ascendant at the same time the progressed Ascendant was conjunct progressed Neptune, lord of the high seas and kidnapping. Mars and Pluto were conjunct in opposition to natal Jupiter, ruler of the ninth house, and Venus was sextile the natal Midheaven. Transiting Uranus was opposing natal Neptune and Neptune was semisquare the progressed Midheaven. The Neptunian nature of this war is clearly seen from the above aspects.

Wellington Defeats Napoleon—June 1815

The war with France had been going on for twenty-two years when Napoleon left Elba and tried to resume power. On a battle-

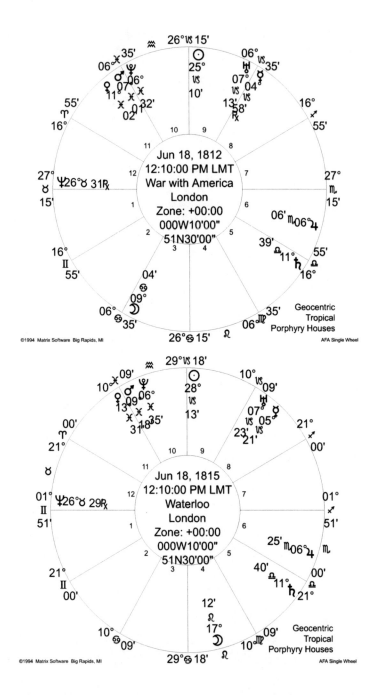

Jun 18, 1812
12:10:00 PM LMT
War with America
London
Zone: +00:00
000W10'00"
51N30'00"

Geocentric
Tropical
Porphyry Houses

©1994 Matrix Software Big Rapids, MI

AFA Single Wheel

Jun 18, 1815
12:10:00 PM LMT
Waterloo
London
Zone: +00:00
000W10'00"
51N30'00"

Geocentric
Tropical
Porphyry Houses

©1994 Matrix Software Big Rapids, MI

AFA Single Wheel

42

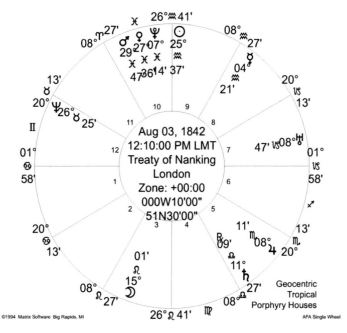

26°♈41'

08°♈27' ☿27' ☿07° ☉25°
29° ♓ ♓ ♒
47°36'14'37'

08°♏27'

04°♏21'

13'♉20' ♆26°♉25'

Ⅱ

01°♋58'

20°♋13'

08°♌27'

26°♌41' ♍

01'♌15°☽

20°♑13'

47'♑08°♅01°♑58'

11'♏09' ♏08°♃20'
11°♎♄27'
08°♎

Aug 03, 1842
12:10:00 PM LMT
Treaty of Nanking
London
Zone: +00:00
000W10'00"
51N30'00"

Geocentric
Tropical
Porphyry Houses

©1994 Matrix Software Big Rapids, MI

AFA Single Wheel

field outside Brussels, he met the Duke of Wellington, who put to rest any future attempts by Napoleon to regain his former glory and empire. This battle would change the face of Europe over the next century after the Treaty of Vienna was signed in late 1815. The progressed Midheaven in the last degree of Capricorn was conjunct natal Venus (ruler of the seventh house), indicative of peace, and sextile the natal Moon. The progressed Sun square the natal Ascendant and Mars sextile the natal Sun gave the English the power and right as victors to exile Napoleon to the island of St. Helena where he died six years later. It was the last time the English would fight against the French: Future conflicts would place them as allies against other nations that threatened world peace.

Transiting Uranus at 4 Sagittarius was square natal Pluto, and Neptune at 22 Pisces was sextile natal Neptune.

The Treaty of Nanking—August 1842

For years the British had been growing opium poppies in India but had little success selling them on the international marketplace. When political instability erupted in China in late 1839, the English

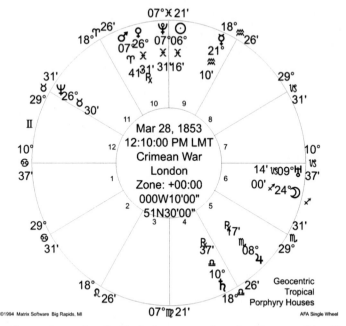

07°♓21'

18°♈26'

♂ ♀ ♆ ☉
07°26° 07°06°
♈ ♓ ♓ ♓
4 131' 31'16'
R

18°♒
☿ 26'
21°
♒
10'

31'
29° ♉
♆26' ♉
30'

Ⅱ
10°
♋
37'

29°
♋
31'

10   9

11

12

Mar 28, 1853
12:10:00 PM LMT
Crimean War
London
Zone: +00:00
000W10'00"
51N30'00"

1

2

3   4

8

7

6

5

29°
♑
31'

10°
♑
37'

14' ♑09°♅
00'♐24°☽

31'
♏

29°

18°
♌26'

♌

18°
R37'
♎
10°
♄

08°♏
4

26'
18°♎

R♏7'

♏
08°

Geocentric
Tropical
Porphyry Houses

©1994 Matrix Software Big Rapids, MI

07°♍21'

AFA Single Wheel

found a ready market for their drugs, much to the dismay of the Chinese. The progressed Sun was square natal Neptune (which rules drugs) when the first Opium War broke out in 1840. Two years later, the Treaty of Nanking ceded Hong Kong to the English, their first colony in the Far East. Progressed Venus square natal Uranus indicated this sudden turn of events while progressed Mars conjunct the natal Moon indicated the force by which the English held onto this colony until the Chinese demanded it back in recent times. The takeover of Hong Kong was somewhat ill-advised due to the nature of the drug situation as shown by Jupiter squaring natal Mars. Saturn squaring the natal Midheaven brought the issue of morality and ethics into the picture as well.

Transiting Uranus at 27 Pisces squared its own position while Neptune at 17 Aquarius, inconjunct Saturn, in some ways pointed to the underhanded manner in which this colony was established.

The Crimean War—March 1853

Disputes arose early in Victoria's reign as to who should control the holy places in Jerusalem, then part of the vast Ottoman Empire

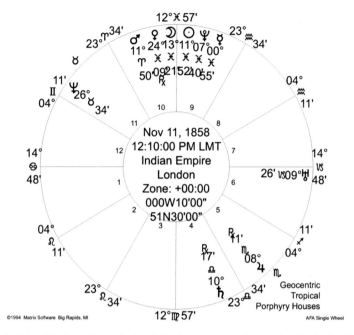

Nov 11, 1858
12:10:00 PM LMT
Indian Empire
London
Zone: +00:00
000W10'00"
51N30'00"

Geocentric
Tropical
Porphyry Houses

©1994 Matrix Software Big Rapids, MI

AFA Single Wheel

ruled by Turkey. Russia had designs on getting a foothold in the Mediterranean, but when its actions became a threat to peace in the area, England sided with France and Turkey against Russia and drove Russian troops across the Black Sea to the Crimean Peninsula. The loss of life for the British was extensive; much of the suffering was alleviated by Florence Nightingale. The progressed Midheaven at 7 Pisces was conjunct progressed Pluto and opposing natal Jupiter, ruler of all things religious. The progressed Ascendant was opposing England's natal Sun and MC, indicating the failure of this campaign for Britain. Mercury square natal Neptune indicated the somewhat misguided nature of this war: Some thought it was fought for commercial reasons rather than for religious supremacy. Mars and Jupiter were sextile their natal positions.

Indian Empire—November 1858

England gained its first foothold on the Indian subcontinent early in the seventeenth century. Bombay was passed to the Crown in 1661 and Calcutta was founded in 1690. After Robert Clive's victory at Plassey in 1757, England controlled the region around

Bihar, Bengal and Orissa. The upper Ganges was subdued two decades later and southern India was brought into British domain by the end of the eighteenth century. The mogul emperor accepted British protection in 1803, thus assuring British sovereignty over the entire region. Britain tried to annex Afghanistan during the 1830s but managed only to gain a foothold in the Punjab. British troops staged a mutiny in 1857 which lasted fourteen months. When the famed Sepoy Mutiny was over, the Mogul Empire was dissolved and control of India was passed from the East India Company to the British Crown. Governing India was a blend of direct and indirect rule: Coastal areas were under direct rule while interior regions were still governed by Maharajahs. England exercised its authority through a viceroy and Victoria was made Empress of India in 1877.

England's progressed Sun and Moon were conjunct its progressed Midheaven while Jupiter sextiled its natal position. Saturn was squaring the natal Sun at the same time Uranus was conjunct that same planet. Both aspects indicated numerous divisions within India which would erupt over the years in hostile conflict, largely between Muslims and Hindus. One must remember that India once consisted of what is now Bangladesh, Pakistan and Burma, as well as India, a region of nearly two million square miles.

Suez Canal—September 1882

When Napoleon conquered Egypt at the end of the eighteenth century, he envisioned a canal across the Isthmus of Suez connecting the Mediterranean with the Red Sea. The French began constructing this canal in 1859 and completed it a decade later. England bought no shares in the canal at first but did later when the Khedive offered up his shares to the British. The canal was vital to British interests in the Far East. The progressed Midheaven at 6 Aries 30 was inconjunct progressed Jupiter (ruler of the ninth house) as well as semisquare natal Neptune, which governs waterways. Venus was sextile England's natal Midheaven, so the transfer of this canal from French to British hands was peaceful. Mars (ruler of the natal Ascendant) was trine natal Uranus (ruler of the eleventh house in the ninth house).

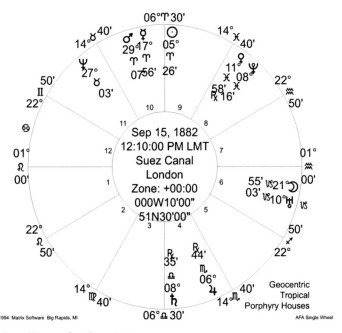

Sep 15, 1882
12:10:00 PM LMT
Suez Canal
London
Zone: +00:00
000W10'00"
51N30'00"

Geocentric
Tropical
Porphyry Houses

The Boer War—October 1899

The Dutch originally settled what was then called the Cape Colony in the mid-seventeenth century but the British waltzed in and took over in 1806. The Boers (native Dutch) fled English rule in 1835, making their Great Trek to the interior and founding the Orange Free State and the Transvaal. When gold was discovered in 1886 near Johannesburg, British settlers rushed in to make their fortunes, further exasperating relations with the Boers, who considered this their territory. A raid led by Jameson in 1895 caused further friction. Futile attempts to reach a peaceful settlement erupted in to a full-scale war in late 1899. The Boers were initially victorious, but after the British captured the capitals of the OFS and Transvaal, the Boers finally surrendered to the British, who then proceeded to make the entire region a colony. When the Boer War began, the Midheaven at 23 Aries sesquisquared natal Jupiter, but as noted before, whenever this degree occupies the Midheaven, part of the problem is religious. Mars at 11 Taurus trined the natal Sun and Midheaven; Uranus was approaching the natal

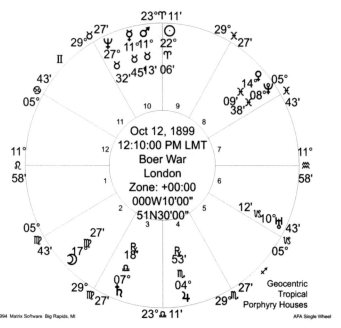

23°♈11'

29°♉27'
ℳ ♂
11°11' ☉
27° 22°
♉ ♉ ♈
32'45'13' 06'

29°♓27'

II

43'
♋
05°

♀ 05°
14°♆ ♓
09°♓ 08° 43'
38'

10   9

11
Oct 12, 1899
12:10:00 PM LMT
12   Boer War
London
1   Zone: +00:00
000W10'00"
2   51N30'00"

8

7

11°
♌
58'

11°
♒
58'

6

3   4

5

12'♑10°♅
05°♑ 43'

05°
♍
43'   27'
☽ 17°♍

18°♅ ℞

53' ℞

07°
♄ ♎

04°
♏
♃

29°♍27'

29°♏27'

vs

♑
05°

♐   Geocentric
Tropical
Porphyry Houses

23°♎11'

©1994 Matrix Software Big Rapids, MI   AFA Single Wheel

Midheaven. Transiting Pluto at 16 Gemini was square natal Saturn and inconjunct Mercury, so British administration over the original settlers would produce further conflicts over the years.

World War I—August 1914

Ever since Germany became an empire in 1871, it had become a threat to the peace within Europe under the rule of Kaiser Wilhelm II, grandson of England's Queen Victoria. Germany allied itself with the vast Austro-Hungarian Empire, so when the heir to that empire was assassinated in the summer of 1914, Germany jumped into the fray to show the world the might of its military industrial complex. When Austria declared war on Serbia, Germany declared war on the rest of Europe. The progressed Midheaven that year was at 7 Taurus 31, within orb of a square to natal Mars, the planet of war. The sextile of the Midheaven to progressed Pluto and the trine to natal Jupiter eventually brought victory for the British, but at a great financial cost, not to mention the tremendous loss of life. At the beginning of the war, England thought it could clean up this mess in a year or so; the progressed Ascendant was squaring natal

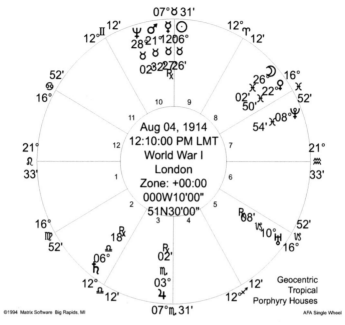

07°♉31'

12°Ⅱ12'   ♆ ♂ ☿ ☉   12°♈12'
28°21'12°06'
♉ ♉ ♉ ♉
02°32'22'26'
R

52'   26°☽16'
☺   02'☽22'♀☓
16°   50'   52'
54'☓08'♇

Aug 04, 1914
21°   12:10:00 PM LMT   7   21°
♌   World War I   ♒
33'   London   33'
Zone: +00:00   6
000W10'00"
51N30'00"

16°   R   52'
♍   18°♃   R♄ 08'   10°♅   16°
52'   06°   02'   ♑
♄   ♏

12°   03°   12°   Geocentric
♎12'   ♃   12'   Tropical
07°♏31'   Porphyry Houses

©1994 Matrix Software Big Rapids, MI   AFA Single Wheel

Neptune, the planet of idealism and misguided aspirations. But their patriotism and self-righteousness were no match for the German army and victory seemed further and further away until the Americans joined the war in mid-1917. Mars conjunct natal Neptune further exacerbated this delusion along with progressed Venus sextile natal Neptune.

It would be the war to end all wars to make Europe safe for democracy, a noble cause but one which the British were ill-prepared to assume. Neptune had now progressed to an inconjunct of natal Uranus indicating the radical nature of this conflict. Craft like the U-Boat (submarine) and flying machines made this the first war fought not only on land and on top of the ocean, but under the seas and overhead. Transiting Uranus at the end of July was at 9 Aquarius, opposite natal Mars, and Neptune at 28 Cancer squared the natal Ascendant, deluding England's ability to win on its own. In November 1918, the armistice with Germany was signed as the Midheaven at 11 Taurus trined its own position: The progressed Ascendant at 24 Leo sesquisquared the natal Sun and progressed Uranus. Never again would England be so sure of its ability to win a

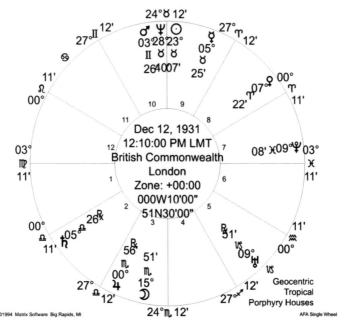

foreign conflict without the aid of its former colony, the United States of America.

The British Commonwealth—December 1931

To ensure that all colonies in the British Empire would be treated fairly, the Commonwealth of Nations was formed when the Statute of Westminster was signed in late 1931. During negotiations, the progressed Midheaven was conjunct natal Neptune and the progressed Ascendant was in early Virgo. England was in the throes of a massive economic depression with considerable unemployment and little hope for its future. The progressed Sun conjunct natal Neptune indicated the desire to dissolve individual differences between the colonies. Transiting Neptune at 8 Virgo was conjunct natal Jupiter; Jupiter occupies the fifth house, which governs colonies—in essence the "children" of the mother country. This position also indicated the British Empire would soon dissolve as one nation after another would demand its freedom and independence. Colonies which went their own way could remain members of the commonwealth only if they acknowledged

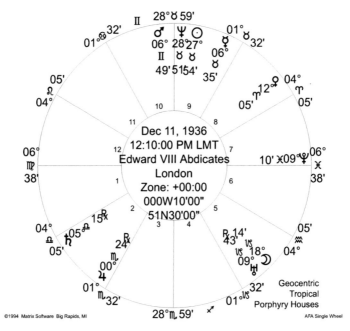

Dec 11, 1936
12:10:00 PM LMT
Edward VIII Abdicates
London
Zone: +00:00
000W10'00"
51N30'00"

Geocentric
Tropical
Porphyry Houses

©1994 Matrix Software Big Rapids, MI

AFA Single Wheel

the monarch as their head of state (Australia and Canada). Other nations like India became republics and elected to remove themselves from British rule.

Abdication of Edward VIII—December 1936

When Edward ascended to the throne early in 1936, he was single and his expected marriage was a cause of great concern. His attraction to American divorcee Wallis Simpson was the source of much gossip in certain circles, but their affair was kept from the British public at the behest of King George V and with the cooperation of the newspapers. When Parliament refused Edward's request to make Wallis his morganatic wife, Edward realized he could not remain on the throne and be married to Wallis, so he abdicated and went into exile in France where he married Wallis the following June. The scandalous nature of their relationship came to a head just as the progressed Midheaven was conjunct progressed Neptune. The Midheaven was also sextile the natal Moon and trine natal Venus, so the British love affair with the former prince of Wales might have caused Parliament to back down if the public had been

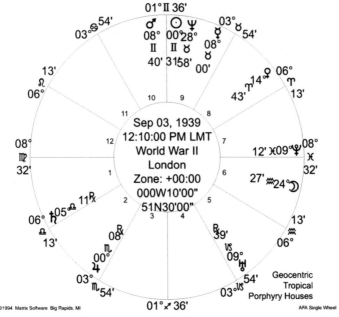

01° II 36'

03° ♋ 54'

♂ 08° II 40' ☉ 00° II 31' ♇ 28° ♉ 58'

03° ♉ 54'

☿ 08° ♉ 00'

13'
06° ♌

10   9

14° ♀ 06°
43' ♈   ♈ 13'

Sep 03, 1939
12:10:00 PM LMT
World War II
London
Zone: +00:00
000W10'00"
51N30'00"

11   8

08° ♍ 32'

12   7

1   6

2   5

3   4

12' ♓ 09° ♅ 08°
♓ 32'

27' ♒ 24° ☽

06° ♎ 13' ♄ 05° ♎ 11° ℞

08° ♏ ℞

00° ♏ 4

03° ♏ 54'

13' ♒
06°

♃ 39' ℞

09° ♑

54' ♑
03° ♑

Geocentric
Tropical
Porphyry Houses

©1994 Matrix Software Big Rapids, MI

01° ♐ 36'

AFA Single Wheel

informed of the affair. But the progressed Midheaven was also inconjunct natal Uranus, bringing the law into the picture. Transiting Pluto at 28 Cancer was squaring England's natal Ascendant and this affair nearly brought down the government while threatening to bring the monarchy to its knees.

World War II—September 1939

Just as England was recovering from Edward's abdication, Hitler annexed Austria and the Sudetenland. Chamberlain made a trip to Munich to visit the German chancellor and returned to England promising "peace in our time." But there was no assuaging Hitler, who signed a non-aggression pact with Stalin to carve up Poland. Shortly thereafter, Hitler invaded Poland and before long had betrayed his partner in crime, Stalin. England's progressed Midheaven had just formed an inconjunct with Jupiter, planet of promises. The Ascendant at 8 Virgo was square progressed Mars and inconjunct natal Mars—two strong indicators of war. The Ascendant was also opposing progressed Pluto, the harbinger of death and annihilation. English spirits were originally high due to the As-

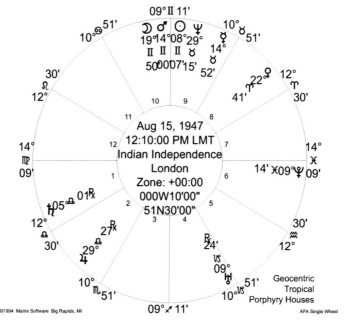

09° ♊ 11'

10° ♋ 51'
10°

☽ ♂ ☉ ♆
19° 14° 08° 29°
♊ ♊ ♊ ♉
50' 00' 07' 15'

10° ♉ 51'
♀
14° ♉
52'

30'
♌
12°

41'
♈ 22° ♀
12°
♈
30'

14°
♍
09'

12
11
10   9
8

Aug 15, 1947
12:10:00 PM LMT
Indian Independence
London
Zone: +00:00
000W10'00"
51N30'00"

7

14°
♓
09'

14' ♓ 09 ♇

1
2
6
3   4   5

♄ 05 ♎ 01 ℞

30'
♒
12°

12°
♎
30'

27 ♎ ℞

♃ 29° ♎

℞
24'

09°
♑
♅ 51'

10°
♏ 51'

10° ♑

Geocentric
Tropical
Porphyry Houses

©1994 Matrix Software Big Rapids, MI

09° ♐ 11'

AFA Single Wheel

cendant's conjunction to natal Jupiter, but again, as in World War I, the German army, navy and air force were simply too much for the English. German planes bombed British cities the following year and laid waste to many shipyards and factories. With progressed Jupiter retrograding to square natal Venus, had the Americans not entered the war, England would have easily lost this conflict. When the war ended in May 1945, the progressed Midheaven at 7 Gemini was square natal Jupiter, the planet of victory. But the end of the war would lead to continued rationing, employment problems and labor strikes over the next few years.

India Granted Independence—August 1947

With the world still recovering from the most devastating holocaust in its history, Britain's empire started to crumble. Problems on the Indian subcontinent (Pakistan and Burma included) as well as in the Middle East (Palestine and Jordan) demanded solutions the English were not prepared to deal with, suffering as they were from the devastation wreaked by the Germans. When the progressed Midheaven at 9 Gemini 11 squared progressed Pluto, India

53

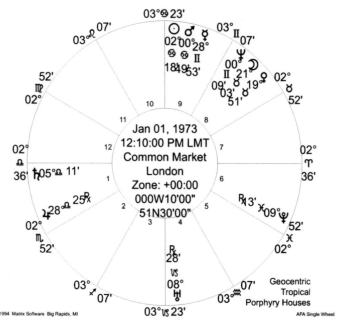

03°♋23'

03°♌07'

52'
♍
02°

02°
♎
36' ♄05°♎11'

♃28°♎ 25°℞

02°
♏
52'

03°♐07'

Jan 01, 1973
12:10:00 PM LMT
Common Market
London
Zone: +00:00
000W10'00"
51N30'00"

☉ ♂ ☿
02°00°28°
♋ ♋ ♊
18'49'53'

03°♊07'

00°♀21°♅
♊ ♄19°♈
09'03'51'
℞

13' ♂
09°♓♇
52'
♓
02°

02°
♉
52'

02°
♈
36'

℞
28'
♑
08°
♅

03°♒07'

03°♑23'

Geocentric
Tropical
Porphyry Houses

©1994 Matrix Software Big Rapids, MI

AFA Single Wheel

was split in two—one Hindu, one Moslem. The progressed Midheaven was also inconjunct England's natal Sun, indicating the loss of prestige and power in the Far East. India remained within the Commonwealth for three and a half years until it became a republic in January 1950. When Palestine was remade into the State of Israel in May 1948, the progressed Sun was exactly square progressed Pluto and the Moon had come to an opposition of natal Uranus in the ninth house. Clearly it was time for the British to withdraw from these areas due to progressed Jupiter's square to natal Venus. Jupiter governs religious issues and Venus rules the natal seventh house of warfare. Religious wars erupted in both regions many years prior to India and Palestine being granted their freedom. As the British saw no quick solution to those dilemmas, they got out in the nick of time.

England Joins the Common Market—January 1973

The idea of a united Europe first surfaced in Napoleon's time when the French emperor envisioned the entire continent under French control. The Treaty of Rome brought that vision into reality in 1957 when the EEC was founded. England opted to join in the mid-1960s but was rebuffed by General DeGaulle. England was finally admitted to the EEC in 1973 but resisted efforts to homogenize its culture. The progressed Midheaven at 3 Cancer was trine natal Pluto while the progressed Ascendant was inconjunct that same planet. Clearly, England could no longer isolate itself if it was to survive economically. The trade pact was not overly popular with the English due to progressed Mercury's square to the Moon, its opposition to natal Uranus in the ninth or the inconjunct to natal Venus, ruler of the seventh house of treaties. Mars, ruler of England's Ascendant, was inconjunct natal Venus as well, indicating the major attitude adjustment the British would have to make in coming years. But there was little England could do as transiting Uranus at 22 Libra was inconjunct Neptune, the planet of resignation and futility. Transiting Pluto at 4 Libra was inconjunct its natal position, demanding massive restructuring of the economy and workforce if England were to compete on the international scene.

The Falklands War—April 1982

British morale had escalated considerably since Margaret Thatcher had become the first woman prime minister in British history. When this feisty female took over in May 1979, the progressed Midheaven was trine natal Jupiter and the progressed Ascendant trined natal Mars. Over the next decade, her fighting spirit would transform the political scene and bring renewed pride to the British people. So, when the Argentines attacked British troops on the Falkland Islands in 1982, the British were incensed and ready to fight. It was simply a matter of national pride: The British wouldn't be pushed into the corner on basic principles. The British government might eventually have given the Islas Malvinas (as they are called in Argentina) back to the Argentines, but with the progressed Ascendant still trine natal Mars and inconjunct progressed Pluto, English troops forced the Argentines to surrender two months later. Venus was trine its natal position, indicating a quick victory. Transiting Neptune at 26 Sagittarius and Pluto at 25 Libra were in aspect to England's natal Ascendant, and the progressed Sun at 11 Cancer was opposing the natal

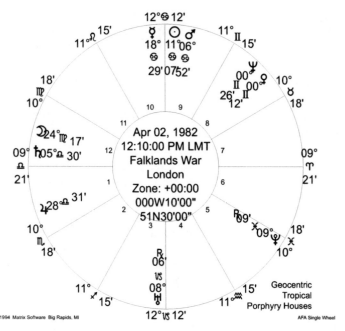

Midheaven. This brief little war put England back in the news in a favorable light and was a spiritual and political turnaround for the nation.

Charles and Diana Separate—December 1992

Nearly a billion people around the world saw Charles, Prince of Wales, marry Diana Spencer in the summer of 1981. Despite the fact their union was an arranged one, they appeared to be content and happily married. Rumors and allegations began to surface in the early 1990s as to the stability of their partnerships and before long the couple was leading separate lives. The Queen did everything in her power to stop the rumors, but three weeks after Windsor Castle burned, she announced the formal separation of her son and his wife. The progressed Midheaven sextile natal Neptune caused innuendo to run rife and other scandals in the royal family also began to surface at this time, most notably among Prince Andrew and his wife Sarah Ferguson, the Duchess of York. Neptune rules scandals and this same planet was prominent in the 1930s when Edward VIII was courting Wallis Simpson. The progressed

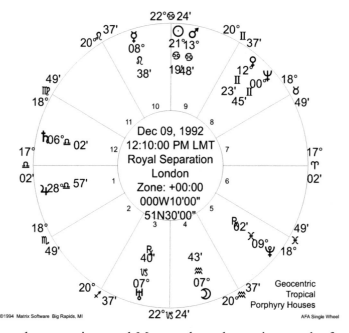

22°♋24'

20°♌37'
☿ 08°
☉ ♂ 21°♋13'
20°♊37'

♋38'
♋ ♋ 19°48'

12°♊
23' ♊
♀ ♇ 18°
00' ♈ 45' ♉ 49'

49'
♍ 18°

10   9

11   8

ħ06°♎02'   12
17° ♎ 02'
♃28°♎57'   1

Dec 09, 1992
12:10:00 PM LMT
Royal Separation
London
Zone: +00:00
000W10'00"
51N30'00"

7   17° ♈ 02'

2   6
3   4   5

18° ♏ 49'

♇02'
♇09' ♓ 18'
49' ♓ 18°

20° ♐37'
♏40'
♑07' ♅
♒07' ☽43'
20°♏37'

22°♑24'

Geocentric
Tropical
Porphyry Houses

©1994 Matrix Software Big Rapids, MI

AFA Single Wheel

Ascendant squaring natal Mercury brought tensions to the fore-front as the tabloid newspapers continued their reign of gossip. Mercury had progressed to form a yod between England's natal Sun and progressed Pluto. Sometimes it seemed as if the tabloids were on a personal mission to destroy the monarchy. Their vitriolic attack was also shown by Mercury's opposition to natal Mars. Transiting Mercury was going over natal Mercury as well during this time, adding even more fuel to an already out of control fire. Transiting Pluto at 22 Scorpio was opposing natal Neptune, indicating the royal breakups and scandals during 1992 which Queen Elizabeth called her annus horibilis, a year she would obviously prefer to forget.

When one looks at the 30° dial, one notes that progressed Mars equals the Moon, Venus and Uranus—not a good augury for domestic bliss or peaceful harmony in marriage.

During the past four decades, the positions of the planets beyond Jupiter have changed little in the English progressed chart. Jupiter is still sextile Uranus (a position it first held in the 1760s), pointing to renewed interest in international matters as Jupiter opposes the natal Ascendant. Like a mutual reception of sorts, progressed Uranus has also been trine natal Jupiter, a position it held in the 1820s when the Industrial Revolution was transforming the British way of life. Transformation is again on the horizon, but this time England will have to cooperate with its neighbors instead of remaining isolated from continental concerns. Progressed Neptune, now in Gemini, is still within orb of sextiling England's natal Moon and trining natal Venus and has been since the end of World War II. Over the past few decades, the British have become more acclimated to the lifestyle of their European neighbors and have resisted less and less the intrusions of foreign customs as this "sceptered isle" has become considerably more cosmopolitan and eclectic in its habits.

Part II
The British Monarchs

William the Conqueror

According to the Bishop of Caen, William I was in his fifty-ninth year when he died on September 9, 1087. He would therefore have been born between September 10, 1028 and September 8, 1029. Most modern historians believe he was born in the autumn of 1028 and according to an ancient medieval manuscript, the Battle of Hastings was fought on his birthday, as William was superstitious and paid attention to both religious and personal holidays. He planned that he should arrive on the south coast of Britain on Michelmas Day at the end of September, a mere fortnight before his birthday, a date that went down in history as the last time this island was successfully invaded.

According to my rectification, William was born in Falaise, France on October 14, 1028 at 5:00 p.m. LAT (4:45 p.m. LMT), the son of Robert, Duke of Normandy, and Herleve, a peasant girl. His parents never married; thus, he was the first Norman monarch known as William the Bastard, a moniker he was none too fond of. His father died in 1035 when Willie was about seven years of age, and he became the Duke of Normandy as his progressed Midheaven trined Saturn (ruler of the Midheaven) and the progressed Ascendant squared the Moon (ruler of the IC).

He married Matilda, daughter of the Earl of Flanders, in 1051 as both his Ascendant and Midheaven were making aspects to Venus,

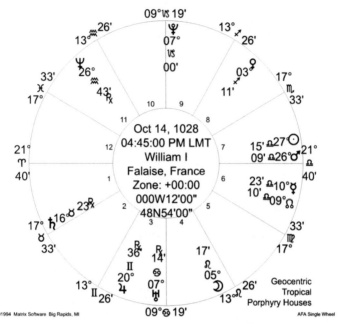

09°♑19'

13°♒26'

Ψ 07° ♑ 00'

13°♐26'

33' ♓ 17°

Ψ 26° ♒ 43' ℞

10   9

♀ 03° 11' ♐

17° ♏ 33'

21° ♈ 40'

12

1

Oct 14, 1028
04:45:00 PM LMT
William I
Falaise, France
Zone: +00:00
000W12'00"
48N54'00"

7

15' ♎27' ☉
09' ♎26° ♂
21° ♎ 40'

2

6

23' ♎10° ☿
10' ♎09°Ω

17° ♉ 33'

♄16° ♉ 23° ℞

3   4   5

33' ♍ 17°

36° ℞ ♅
♊ 20° ♃

14° ℞ ☊ 07° ♋

17' Ω 05°

13° ♊ 26'

09°♋19'

☽ 13°Ω26'

Geocentric
Tropical
Porphyry Houses

©1994 Matrix Software Big Rapids, MI

AFA Single Wheel

ruler of his Descendant. William and Matilda met in the heat of passion; for some strange reason, when he laid eyes on her, he tore off her clothes, flung her down in the street, slapped her face and rode away. Talk about strange courting procedures! They were married five years later. Physically, they were the original "odd couple"; he stood 5'10" tall, while she was 4'2", her mouth coming up only to his belly button. But they had a happy life together, producing four sons and six daughters. Due to the fact that they were cousins, the Pope excommunicated them, an act that was later rescinded when they agreed to build a religious edifice. Amazing how money talks, isn't it? William was completely faithful to Matilda and never took a mistress, which was very unusual in those days when royals bedded whomever they wanted.

The same year they were married, Edward the Confessor, King of England, promised his cousin William the throne as he had no heir. Note that Venus also rules the second house of wealth as well as the seventh house of alliances. So when Edward died early in 1066, William was surprised he was not asked to rule. The barons chose Harold, thus laying the stage for William's invasion later that year. As William's progressed Ascendant was conjuncting Jupiter, he felt he couldn't lose, so preparations were made to claim his inheritance. Landing at Pevensey on September 28, he rode inland a bit and met Harold on the battle field at Hastings on October 14, his birthday, according to my calculations. Two months later, he was crowned in London, beginning a dynasty that has ruled England for more than nine centuries. During the coronation, a loud cry went up inside, and the soldiers outside thought there was trouble. In panic, they set fire to several houses near the church. William consolidated his power over the next five years and built numerous castles, such as the Tower of London, to protect his domain.

William's wife Matilda died in 1083 just as his progressed Midheaven was inconjunct the Moon. Three years later, a massive survey of his land holdings, known as the Domesday Book, was finished as the Midheaven trined Uranus. A year later, he prepared for battle against the King of France, who had insulted him, probably calling him a "fat bastard" or something similar. During the conflict, William's horse fell on top of him and gored his groin: He died at sunrise on September 9, 1087 in Rouen, the capital of Normandy. While his body was being carried to the burial site, the coffin burst and the contents spilled over the pavement. The stench was overwhelming and several of the mourners were overcome. The progressed Ascendant was opposing Pluto, ruler of his eighth house, which also led to fights and arguments among his surviving male heirs. His holdings were to be divided thus: Robert Curthose was to receive Normandy, despite the fact that his eldest son was William's enemy at the time and was on friendly terms with the King of France; his second son, William II, got the crown of England; and his youngest, Henry, received the sum of 5,000 pounds but no land.

Pluto at William's Midheaven made him a stern ruler, an autocrat who often was merciless and vengeful toward his enemies. The ruler of his Midheaven, Saturn, occupied the sign of Taurus, known as the builder, while Mars, ruler of his Ascendant, sits in the seventh house conjunct the Sun, bringing him victory over his enemies. Note that Jupiter, ruler of the ninth house, trines the Sun-Mars conjunction; thus, through successful foreign intervention, he changed forever the workings and lifestyle of England. But with

Saturn rising, he was shrewd and wise enough not to disturb too many Saxon institutions; he proceeded slowly and cautiously at first until his authority was secure.

Having the Sun conjunct Mars gave William a powerful physique even though he became quite corpulent in later years. In his personal life, William was pious, temperate and respected as well as feared. William loved his children dearly, shown by the Sun (ruler of the fifth) trine Jupiter, as well as the Moon trine Venus. His short hair was unusual for his time; other monarchs wore their tresses long, with flowing beards.

Comparing William's natal chart to the moment he was crowned King of England on Christmas Day 1066, we note his natal Pluto conjunct the transiting Sun and Midheaven, which was sextile transiting Pluto and trine Jupiter. Neptune has moved to a square of its own position, while his Saturn trined its own position. William's Sun and Mars opposed the coronation Ascendant and his Moon opposed the coronation Mars.

Henry I

Unfortunately, no birth date is known for William the Conqueror's successor, William II. He was born in France about 1058 and was known as Rufus due to his ruddy complexion and red hair. His reign was one of decadence and licentiousness, largely due to his homosexual inclinations. He reigned from 1087 until 1100.

His brother, Henry I, was born September 20, 1068 in Selby, England at 4:30 p.m. (4:22 p.m. LMT) according to my rectification of date and time. His mother, Matilda of Flanders, died in September 1087 (Midheaven conjunct Uranus square Saturn; Ascendant opposition Sun and Saturn). On August 2, 1100, his brother, William II, was "accidentally" shot while on a hunting expedition. Many thought Henry had a hand in his brother's death, for within three days he had looted the national treasury and had himself crowned (Midheaven square Jupiter sesquisquare Neptune). Three months later he married Edith, who was the daughter of Malcolm III of Scotland. She took the name of Mathilde.

In 1101, his brother, Robert, the Duke of Normandy, invaded England trying to usurp his younger brother (Ascendant inconjunct Mars). The brothers made a temporary peace until Robert again

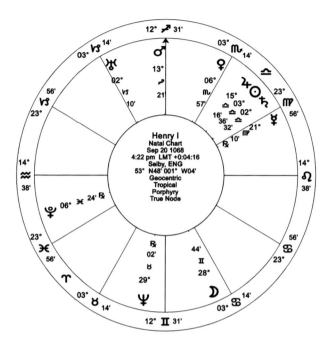

Henry I
Natal Chart
Sep 20 1068
4:22 pm LMT +0:04:16
Selby, ENG
53° N48' 001° W04'
Geocentric
Tropical
Porphyry
True Node

went to war against Henry I in 1106. This time Henry ousted Robert and took Normandy for himself (Midheaven trine Mercury semisquare Pluto; Ascendant trine Mercury). In 1118, his wife, Mathilde, died (Midheaven trine Sun and Saturn) and two years later, his heir, Prince William, drowned while attempting to return to England (Midheaven sesquisquare Mercury; Ascendant opposition Mars). His daughter, Matilda, thus became his heir. Henry married Adela of Louvain in January 1121, but their union left no legitimate heirs to the throne (Midheaven square Venus; Ascendant trine Jupiter). Henry died of food poisoning on December 1, 1135 (Ascendant conjunct Moon).

Henry was well educated and a fine scholar, hence his nickname of Beauclerc. Despite the fact that he was more placid and sober than his predecessors, he could be harsh, strict and ruthless (Sun conjunct Saturn square Uranus). Henry also was called the "Lion of Justice" for his numerous legal reforms, such as the Curia Regis. Henry also reformed taxation procedures and established England's first civil bureaucracy. Henry was also quite a ladies' man; he sired 24 children, all but three of them illegitimate. Was it that Moon in Gemini (ruling the fifth house) opposite Uranus? Upon his death of food poisoning on December 1, 1135, his only heir was his daughter, Matilda, and her husband, Geoffrey Plantagenet, from whom Henry II was descended.

But Matilda was not to rule. That honor went instead to Stephen of Blois, son of Adela, daughter of William the Conqueror. Matilda didn't take this lying down and vowed to fight for her rights. Thus did a civil war erupt in 1139 that lasted for three years. One month before Stephen's death in December 1154, Henry Plantagenet was named the future King of England.

The Plantagenets

Henry II

Henry Plantagenet was born in Le Mans, France on March 5, 1133 at 2:00 p.m. LAT (2:10 p.m. LMT) according to my rectification. His father, Geoffrey Plantagenet, was born August 24, 1113, with the Sun in Virgo and the Moon in Capricorn. His mother, eleven years older than her husband, was born in 1102 and was the daughter of Henry I of England. Her first marriage at age twelve was to the Holy Roman Emperor, Henry V, who was 16 years her senior. She was a widow at age 23 and five years later married Geoffrey, Count of Anjou and Maine. When her father died in 1135, she tried to claim the throne and four years later provoked a civil war. She was crowned Queen of England in 1141 and for a time usurped the throne from her cousin Stephen. Matilda was a proud and arrogant woman, haughty and domineering, but a strategist of the first order. So even though she could not become Queen of England in her own right, her son won the honor.

Henry's father died in September 1151 as his progressed Midheaven was conjunct Pluto. On May 18, 1152 he married Eleanor of Aquitaine, the richest woman in Europe, who was ten years his senior. Eleanor was a feminist, a woman in her own right who had married Louis VII, the King of France, when she was fifteen. I've erected a speculative chart for her, giving her a Libra Sun and

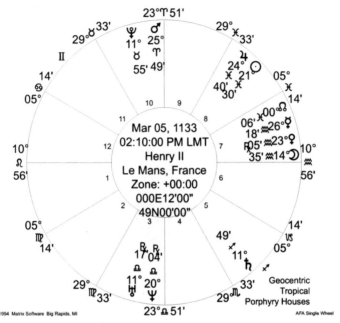

23°♈51'

29°♉33'

II

14'
♋
05°

10°
♌
56'

05°
♍
14'

29°♍33'

♅ ♂
11° 25°
♉ ♈
55' 49'

Mar 05, 1133
02:10:00 PM LMT
Henry II
Le Mans, France
Zone: +00:00
000E12'00"
49N00'00"

R R
17°04'
♎ ♎
11° 20°
♅ ♆

23°♎51'

29°♓33'

24°
♓ 21° ☉
40' ♓ 05°
30' ♓
14'

06'♓00°♌
18'♒26°☿
05'♒23°♀
35'♒14°☽10°
56'

14'
♑
49' 05°
✶
11°
♄ ♐

29°♏33'

10
9
11
8
12
7
1
6
2
5
3
4

Geocentric
Tropical
Porphyry Houses

©1994 Matrix Software Big Rapids, MI

AFA Single Wheel

Cancer Moon with Aquarius rising. Eleanor was an independent spirit, never afraid to be assertive, due to the Sun conjunct Mars. She retained control of her own life due to Pluto squaring her Ascendant and was known to be quite charming and intelligent. She lived a life of sophistication and elegance, was high spirited and quick witted and could be extravagant and easily bored due to the squares to her Moon. Eleanor put great value on wealth and power due to those eighth house positions and she was restless and lacked discipline. She couldn't stand restrictions of any kind and was quite impatient to see immediate results.

Eleanor's life reads like a soap opera. Born in Bordeaux on September 24, 1122 at 3:30 p.m. LAT (3:20 p.m. LMT), her mother died when she was eight as the Ascendant opposed Uranus. Her father died seven years later and she inherited the vast domain of Aquitaine as the Ascendant sextiled Pluto. Three months later, in July 1137, she married Louis VII and became the Queen of France. It was a marriage of opposites, her wild lifestyle contrasting sharply with her husband's monk-like existence. She decided to join her husband, however, on the Second Crusade in June 1147

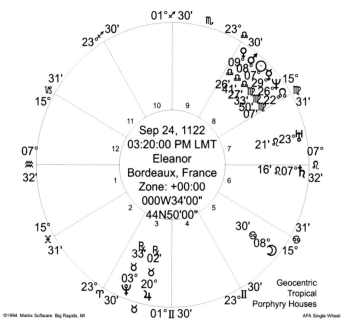

and formed the Queen's Guard to accompany her. Eleanor's progressed Midheaven was squaring Neptune, indicative of one problem after another. Landing in Constantinople, she was impressed by its oriental artifacts, especially silk. Her entourage was ambushed by Turks two months before arriving in Antioch as the Ascendant opposed Neptune and her Sun opposed Pluto. Her ventures in the Holy Land continually frustrated her; she departed for France a year later after trying to get her husband to divorce her. She should have known better as her Midheaven was squaring Mercury. Her second daughter was born the following year, but after protracted negotiations, the King agreed to give her a divorce just as her Sun squared Saturn. She was divorced in March 1152 and two months later married Henry II, her Midheaven now sextile Pluto and her Ascendant trine Saturn. Their union was obviously based on a strong chemical reaction, for their lovemaking was highly passionate and intense and little was left to the imagination. She was five months pregnant at the altar, a scandal to everyone on the Continent except the French, of course.

Her first child, also named Henry, was born in 1153 as the Ascendant squared the Sun; he lived only three years. Another child, also named Henry, was born in February 1155 and would be come charming and unpredictable like his mother. As Queen of England since December 1154 (progressed Ascendant square Moon opposed Mars), the combined estates of Eleanor and her husband were immense, occupying most of France and all of England. She bore Henry two future kings: Richard in 1157, who would become a warrior and poet, and John in 1167, who was shameless, crafty and ungrateful. Tired of Henry's repeated affairs, Eleanor left for her homeland a year later just as her Ascendant was inconjunct the Sun and square Saturn. There, in Poitiers, she established what was to become known as the Court of Love, where women were superior to men and the troubadours sang songs of praise to the "weaker sex." She conspired against her husband Henry in the spring of 1173 with her sons Henry, Richard and Geoffrey. One year later, she was captured and imprisoned with the Midheaven inconjunct Uranus and the Sun occupying the twenty-ninth degree of Scorpio.

Her son Henry died in June 1183 (Midheaven square Pluto) and her son Geoffrey was killed in an accident three years later (progressed Midheaven opposed Saturn). When her husband Henry II died in July 1189, she was finally released from prison on orders from her son Richard (Midheaven trine Mars, Ascendant trine Sun). During her son's reign, she played matchmaker for him and raised the ransom to release him from prison in Austria. Richard died in her arms in April 1199 (progressed Midheaven square Jupiter); five years later, on April 11, 1204, Eleanor died at the Abbey at Fontevraud at age 81. Her Sun was square Mercury (ruler of her fourth and eighth houses), her Midheaven opposed Uranus (ruler of her Ascendant) and the Ascendant was semisquare Saturn (ruler of the twelfth and co-ruler of the Ascendant).

But back to Henry. When he married Eleanor, his progressed Ascendant opposed Venus; when he became king of England in December 1154, the Midheaven was squaring the Moon and the Ascendant was inconjunct Jupiter, ruler of good fortune. Leo rising gave him great strength, red hair, and a short and stocky build. With Mars at the Midheaven, Henry had a violent temper and boundless physical energy,. The legendary Plantagenet outbursts of temper were seemingly inherited: Some even believed they were possessed of the devil himself and the entire family was insane. Being a Pisces, Henry was overly emotional to begin with, and with the sign of kingship on the Ascendant, he brooked any attempt that mitigated his authority.

One of the biggest fights of his early reign involved his friend Thomas Becket, whom Henry had made Chancellor of England. Henry thought that with his friend in such a high position, he could get away with matters much more easily. But Henry made the mistake of making his friend Archbishop of Canterbury in June 1162. He hadn't counted on Becket suddenly becoming pious, and arguments between them over the rights of clergymen to be tried in civil courts erupted into open warfare. At his wits' end, Henry finally said, "Will no one rid me of this turbulent priest?" Four of his henchmen took his musing seriously. Becket was murdered in Canterbury Cathedral before the altar on December 29, 1170, eight days after his fifty-second birthday. England was horrified and the Pope forced Henry to do penance by walking barefoot through Canterbury in pilgrim's robes. He then bared his back to monks, who flogged him. It was the ultimate humiliation for such a proud man. Fifteen months after Becket's death, the former friend of Henry's was canonized by the church. Becket's tomb was the sight of many pilgrimages during the Middle Ages and its upkeep was entrusted to the crown in perpetuity. During this time Henry's progressed Sun was at 29 Aries, squaring his Neptune/Pluto midpoint.

The following year, in 1171, Henry conquered Ireland, thus beginning the enmity between the people of that island and their English overlords that remains to this day. In March 1173, soldiers loyal to Henry captured his wife, who was planning a revolt against her husband with the aid of her sons Henry, Richard and Geoffrey, who were under protection from the King of France. Rebellion ensued when Prince Henry (born in 1155) grew tired and impatient of having little real power and practically nothing to do. His father had crowned him King of England three years earlier to ensure the succession. But little Henry also hated to part with his lands to his little brother John, so open warfare was the result. Eleanor was captured the following year and imprisoned until Henry's death fifteen years later.

Henry's eldest surviving son, Henry, died in 1183, thus making

Richard his heir (progressed Midheaven opposed Saturn). Henry died on July 6, 1189 in the castle of Chinon, an embittered man. Betrayed by his sons, his empire in ruins, and forced to submit to his arch-enemy the King of France, when he received the news that even his youngest son John had turned against him, he was vanquished once and for all and lost the will to live. When his son Richard viewed the corpse, blood oozed from Henry's nostrils, a bad omen to superstitious people in those days. According to some, a corpse was said to bleed in the presence of its murderer. Henry's progressed Ascendant was opposite the Sun, ruler of his natal Ascendant.

During his reign, despite the personal battles with his wife and family, Henry managed to centralize the government. Very stern and ambitious due to Saturn trining the Ascendant, his ruthless and ignominious end may also be shown by Pluto squaring the Ascendant. Henry's conflict with the church is shown by the ruler of the ninth house (Neptune) in opposition to Mars (ruler of the Midheaven). His continual fights with his male offspring are shown by Saturn in the fifth house; some say he had little affection for his brood, who eventually went to war against him as shown by Saturn's sesquisquare Mars and inconjunct Pluto. Hated by his wife due to Uranus inconjunct Pluto, his daughters did manage to marry into the ruling houses of Sicily, Castile and Saxony. In the end, Henry was undone by those whom he loved most, a sad legacy for such a proud and powerful man.

Richard I

Richard was born in Oxford, England on September 8, 1157. According to Martin Harvey in his book *Nativitas*, Richard was born at night. An old medieval biography gave the time of 3:00 a.m. LAT (2:55 a.m. LMT), which I will use here. He was betrothed to Alice at age twelve when his progressed Midheaven trined the Sun, but it was an exercise in futility as the future king was homosexual and had little interest in women. His mother made him the Duke of Aquitaine in 1172 (progressed Ascendant conjunct Venus, ruler of the Midheaven), in effect making him the richest landowner in Europe. One year later, along with his brothers Henry and Geoffrey, he joined forces against his father at the behest of his mother who

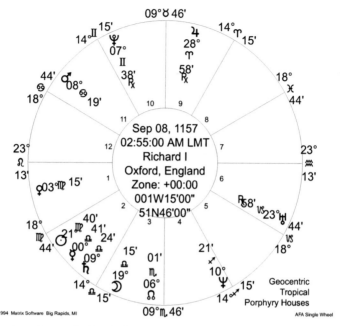

09° ♉ 46'

14° ♊ 15'

♇ 07° ♊ 38' ℞

09° ♉ 46'

14° ♈ 15'

♃ 28° ♈ 58' ℞

18° ♓ 44'

44' ♂ 08° ♋ 19'
18° ♋

23° ♌ 13'

♀ 03° ♍ 15'

10   9

11   8

12   Sep 08, 1157   7
02:55:00 AM LMT
Richard I
1   Oxford, England   6
Zone: +00:00
2   001W15'00"   5
51N46'00"
3   4

23° ♒ 13'

℞ 58' ♑ 23° ♅ 44'

18° ♍ 44'   ♂ 21 ♍ 41'
♀ 00° ♎ 24'
♄ 09°

15'   ♎ 01'
19° ♏ 06'
☽ 15'   ☊

21'   ♐
10°

18° ♑ 44'

14° ♎

14° ♏ 15'

14 ♏ 15'
♆

Geocentric
Tropical
Porphyry Houses

©1994 Matrix Software Big Rapids, MI

AFA Single Wheel

was imprisoned the following year (progressed Ascendant semisquare the Moon). With the death of his elder brother Henry in 1183, Richard became the heir to the throne, a *fait accompli* after the death of his father six years later (progressed Midheaven semisquare Jupiter).

During his ten-year reign he spent only six months in England, preferring to devote his time to conquering the Holy Land from the infidels, shown by Jupiter in the ninth house trine the Ascendant. His role in the Crusades earned him the popular name of Richard the Lion-Hearted. His absence from England could also be shown by the fact that when he was crowned, his progressed Midheaven was also opposing Neptune in his fourth house. That placement often indicates a person for whom the entire world is home, and that individual never really feels tied to any one place. Besides, in Jerusalem Richard's relocated Midheaven trined his Moon and his Sun was close to the relocated Ascendant. In order to finance his Crusade, Richard sold nearly everything in sight. One of his most profitable ventures involved the granting of charters to English towns; thus did many communities begin their legal history under his reign. Richard left for the Holy Land in mid-1190 with his lover Philip Augustus, the King of France, but they failed to take Jerusalem two years later. On his journey east, his mother had found Richard a suitable wife, Berengaria of Navarre, who was eight years his junior. They were married in Sicily, but due to Richard's sexual leanings, had no children. She returned to the Aquitaine in 1192 and never set foot in England.

Disgruntled at failing to capture Jerusalem, Richard left for England after hearing that his brother John was plotting a coup even though Eleanor was technically regent during his absence. Traveling overland, he was captured by Duke Leopold, whom he had insulted on the Crusade. He was held for a ransom of 100,000 marks by the Holy Roman Emperor from December 1192 until he was released in February 1194. He was found by the minstrel Blondel, who sang him songs from outside the castle walls. During his stint in prison, Richard's progressed Sun was semisquare Neptune and eventually opposed Jupiter on his release. It was a sad time for him, but upon his return to England he forgave his brother John and was crowned a second time.

Always searching for fame and glory to the end, he journeyed to Chalus in France in the spring of 1199 upon hearing that a cache of gold lay nearby, possibly the site of an old Roman treasure house. He died during the siege on April 6, 1199 at 7:00 p.m. of a crossbow wound that quickly became gangrenous. As he left no heir, the throne went to his brother John.

Richard was the stuff of which legends are made. Always the consummate medieval hero and knight in shining armor, he was tall and fair haired, with blue eyes and mucho charisma. His life was glamorous and dashing, his intellectual and musical abilities inherited from his mother. Leo rising made him an egotist, always self-confident and seldom afraid of anything. His martial interests, as well as his fierce temper, are shown by Mars semisquare the Ascendant, while his lack of interest in politics is shown by Saturn semisquare the Ascendant. Thus was the Ascendant the midpoint of Mars/Saturn. His love life might be shown by Uranus (ruler of the Descendant) square the Moon (rules women in general) and Jupiter (ruler of his fifth house of pleasure). The conflicts with his father are shown by Pluto (ruler of the IC) opposing Neptune in the fourth house and both of them square Venus, ruler of the Midheaven. His troubles over his brother John are aptly illustrated by those Venus squares as well as the Moon in the third house semisquare Venus and square Uranus, ruler of the Descendant. Thus would siblings become open enemies. Ironically, he remained close to his mother, possibly due to his Moon conjunct her Sun. John's Moon-Mars opposition and Venus-Jupiter conjunction negatively aspected Richard's rising degree. Obviously they had little love for each other for they were worlds apart temperamentally, physically and morally.

John

John was born on Christmas Eve 1167 in Oxford, England. According to Martin Harvey's *Nativitas*, he was born between sundown and the end of twilight, which took place two hours later. I've chosen the time of 4:00 p.m. LAT (4:04 p.m. LMT) as the earlier time suits the life of the youngest child of Henry and Eleanor much better. His parents separated before he was a year old, John going to France with his mother. Because his parents divided their estates with his older brothers, John ended up with nothing, hence the nickname "Lackland." Shortly after the death of his brother Henry in 1183, John was sent to Ireland to maintain the peace, but his mission failed miserably even though his progressed Midheaven trined Mars. It seems the baby of the family could do nothing right and couldn't be trusted one bit. When his brother Richard died in 1189, his mother was made regent in his brother's absence, which John didn't take lying down. Because John was plotting a coup in 1192, Richard rushed home through the heart of Europe and was captured and held for ransom. John's mother had to bail her son Richard out of jail because of John's impertinence and lack of loyalty.

Upon his brother's ascension to the throne, John had married Hadwiga (or Isabel) of Gloucester, the wealthiest heiress in England, just as his progressed Midheaven sextiled Saturn, co-ruler of his Descendant. Ten years later, after producing no children, he divorced his wife shortly after becoming king. John's progressed aspects that year were the Ascendant opposing Saturn and inconjunct Neptune, while the progressed Midheaven was semisquare the Moon and sesquisquare Mars. With aspects like that, it's no wonder

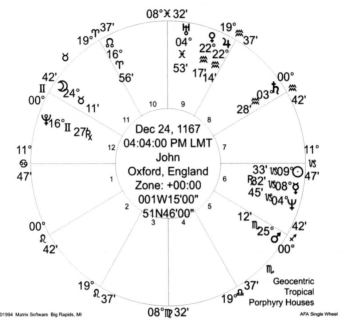

08°✶ 32'

19°♈37'
19°♈︎ ♌︎ 16° ♈︎ 56'
☿ 04° ✶ 53' ♀ 22° ♄ 22° ♒︎ 37' 17° ♒︎ 14'

42' ♃ 24° ♉︎ 11'
II 00°
♆ 16° II 27℞
11° ♋︎ 47'

00° ♌︎ 42'
19° ♌︎ 37'

08°♍ 32'

28' ♄ 03° ♒︎ 00° 42'

33' ♑09°☉ 47'
℞32' ♑08°☿ 45' ♑04°♆ 42'
♏25°♂ 12' ♐
00°
♏

19°♎ 37'

11° ♑ 47'

Dec 24, 1167
04:04:00 PM LMT
John
Oxford, England
Zone: +00:00
001W15'00"
51N46'00"

10 9 8 7 6 5 4 3 2 1 12 11

Geocentric
Tropical
Porphyry Houses

©1994 Matrix Software Big Rapids, MI

AFA Single Wheel

his reign was fraught with so much tension and animosity. One year later, in 1200, John met Isabelle of Angouleme, a girl of only fourteen who was betrothed to Hugh Lusignan. Caring not one whit for the fact that she was promised to another man, he abducted her. During the marriage ceremony, she wept incessantly; nevertheless, she produced two sons and three daughters before she grew bored. Once she took a lover and when John discovered the deed, he killed him and hung his corpse over his wife's bed. Ironically, upon her husband's death, Isabelle returned to France where four years later she married Lusignan, her initially betrothed.

As previously stated, Richard inherited the Aquitaine while his elder brother Henry received Normandy. Arthur, son of his brother Geoffrey, held sway in Brittany. John made war on his nephew and some think he had Arthur murdered to gain his territory. We may never know as his progressed Ascendant was inconjunct Neptune. Four years later, John had lost most of his French estates as his progressed Midheaven sextiled Pluto. But John had other trouble on his hands due to a dispute over who should become the Archbishop of Canterbury. The fight brewed for several years until 1208 when the Pope placed an interdict on the entire nation of England. One year later, John was excommunicated as his Midheaven semisquared Uranus (ruler of the ninth house) and the Ascendant was inconjunct the Sun. The Pope finally recanted and annulled the excommunication even though John was a reputed agnostic and had expropriated all church property in the meantime. John had become a vassal of the Pope by 1213, but he was making enemies elsewhere.

The barons had been plotting against John for years, accusing him of seducing their wives, among other things. The barons met at Runnymede near Windsor on June 15, 1215 and forced John to sign their charter of liberties known as the Magna Carta. Taxes would be curbed and the barons' properties would be protected as well as their privileges. It said no free man could be arrested, imprisoned or exiled without the judgment of his peers, a concept that appeared much later in the U.S. Bill of Rights. Returning home from the signing, John foamed at the mouth and went into a frenzy. He broke his word, which he had never intended to live up to—typical of this man who became so universally reviled. Often in his state of madness he bit things or people and set fire to anything close at hand.

John's desire was as ignominious as the beginning of his reign. During his coronation ceremony, he dropped his ducal banner and had to stoop to recover it. In October 1216, while fleeing the barons who forced him into submission, John's baggage train was caught in the quicksand in the Wash (an arm of the North Sea) and the entire royal treasury of crown jewels was lost as the tide swept in from the sea. John's progressed Ascendant was sextile Pluto, placed natally in his twelfth house of self-undoing.

John had been a short, stocky kid who bore little of the regal nature of his illustrious parents. Despite the fact that he was quite well read and even brilliant at times, his greed and treachery overshadowed his finer traits. John's T-square involving four planets in fixed signs which aspect his natal Ascendant gave him a weighty cross to bear. His violent temper and harsh cruelty may be shown by the Moon-Mars opposition. The fact he was betrayed and also betrayed those closest to him is shown by the ruler of the eleventh house (Mars) being a part of the T-square and the Moon occupying the eleventh house as well.

John's adoration of his father is illustrated by Neptune conjunct Mercury (ruler of the IC), but despite that fact, John turned against his father in due time as the Sun-Mercury conjunction also feeds into the horrible T-square. The problems with his brother Richard could be shown as well by the ruler of the third house (the Sun) being semisquare Venus, Jupiter and Mars, while his lack of territory and nickname Lackland are shown by Saturn occupying the eighth house of inheritance. John's problems with the church came from the Aquarius duo in the ninth house squaring the ruler of his Ascendant, the Moon. John trusted no one and nobody trusted him—a Capricorn trait he played to the hilt. With the ruler of his Sun sign (Saturn sesquisquare Pluto in the twelfth house), lessons from his reign were well remembered in future years when the barons created the first Parliament.

Henry III

Henry III was born in Winchester, England on October 1, 1207 at 3:30 a.m. according to an article in *American Astrology* (I've rectified the birth time to 3:24 a.m. LAT). Henry became king at age nine, following the death of his father King John. Since the crown jewels had been lost at sea, Henry's mother's bracelet was used as a makeshift crown (progressed Midheaven trine Sun). Coronation robes were also improvised and the young king was crowned by the Bishop of Winchester because the Archbishop of Canterbury was away in Rome. From his father's misrule, Henry inherited a bankrupt kingdom with no central government. Four years later, Henry's mother married Hugh Lusignan, her first fiancé, and Henry's domestic life assumed a continental atmosphere. Henry's preference for foreigners over Englishmen caused quite a stir at court and in 1234 he was forced to remove many who held high office (progressed Midheaven square Neptune).

Henry married Eleanor of Provence, sister to the Queen of France, in January 1236. Eleanor was a strikingly beautiful woman fifteen years younger than Henry. Their courtship began after Eleanor had written a poem and sent it to Henry's younger brother. Henry was so impressed by the poem that he asked to meet its author. Note that Neptune sits in his seventh house of marriage and his progressed Ascendant was opposing that planet when he married.

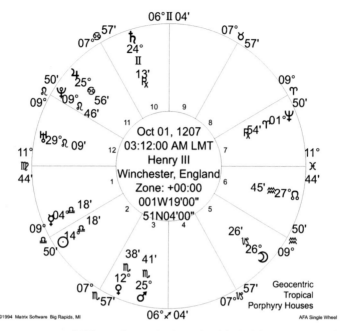

06° II 04'

07° ⊗ 57'

ħ 24° II 13' ℞

07° ♉ 57'

50' ♃ 25° ⊗
09° ♀ 09' Ω 56' 46'

09° ♈ 50'

10 | 9

11

8

Oct 01, 1207
03:12:00 AM LMT
Henry III
Winchester, England
Zone: +00:00
001W19'00"
51N04'00"

♅ 29° Ω 09'
11° ♍ 44'

12

7

1

6

2

5

3 | 4

♇ 54' ♈ 01° ♆
11° ♓ 44'

45' ♒ 27° ☊

♀ 04° ♎ 18' 18'
09° ♎ 50'
⊙ 4° ♎

26'
♑ 26° ☽

50'
♒ 09'

07° ♏ 57'
♏ 57'

♏ 12° ♏ 25°
♀ 38' 41' ♂

07° ♑ 57'

Geocentric
Tropical
Porphyry Houses

©1994 Matrix Software Big Rapids, MI

06° ✶ 04'

AFA Single Wheel

Henry renovated Westminster Palace for his bride; to ensure her warmth, he installed many huge fireplaces. Their union was a real love match from its inception.

Henry's mother, Isabella of Angouleme, died in 1246 (progressed Midheaven square Sun semisquare Uranus). Due to various internal squabbles, in 1259 Henry renounced all claims to the French provinces of Normandy, Anjou and Maine a year after being forced to sign the Provisions of Oxford at the behest of the nobles. It seems that Henry was following in his father's dictatorial footsteps. By spring 1264, Henry was close to provoking a civil war. Battle lines were drawn and the Earl of Leicester, Simon de Montfort, came close to taking over the country. In 1264, Montfort was killed in battle by Henry's son Edward (progressed Midheaven sextile Mercury; Ascendant square Moon and Jupiter). England's first parliament met later that year.

Henry died on November 16, 1272 at age 65 (progressed Midheaven square Venus; Ascendant inconjunct Neptune) and as promised, his heart was removed and sent to the Abbess of Fontevraud.

Henry was a pious man, highly critical and with an eye for detail (Virgo Ascendant). He was a simple man with genuine concern for the common folk. Some called his lack of interest in the martial activities a sign of cowardice. He lacked sound judgment and was often inconsistent in his dealings with others (Libra Sun and Mercury with Neptune in the seventh house). He was fickle, untrustworthy and indecisive. However, he was generous to his friends (Moon opposite Jupiter) and showed natural good taste as he redecorated royal residences with the best finery available (Libra Sun and Mercury). Seldom commanding respect (possibly Saturn in the tenth house inconjunct Mars), he is largely remembered for ruling over a period of English history ripe with artistic and intellectual achievements.

Edward I

According to most sources, including a biography by Prestwick, Edward was born in London on June 17, 1239, very late at night. I've rectified the time to 11:15 p.m. LAT (11:17 p.m. LMT). In October 1254 (age fifteen) he entered an arranged marriage with Eleanor (age ten), daughter of the King of Castile (progressed Midheaven opposite Venus; progressed Ascendant opposite Pluto). It was a happy and fruitful union which generated fifteen children. The couple left on a Crusade to the Holy Land in 1270 (Midheaven trine Mars; Ascendant trine Uranus) and while there learned of the death of Edward's father (Midheaven sextile Jupiter; Ascendant trine Mars). Edward and Eleanor spent a lengthy four years overseas, not arriving home until August 1274.

Edward earned a reputation as a legal reformer (Sagittarius Midheaven with Jupiter in the first house). Rather than introducing new concepts, Edward codified statutes already in effect. He began to consolidate his power and authority over all the British Isles. Wales was first to feel his demands and by 1284 was completely conquered (Midheaven inconjunct Venus).

His beloved queen died in late 1290. Edward commemorated her by placing a cross at each of the 12 spots her funeral cortege rested overnight on its journey from Nottinghamshire to London. The most famous memorial is Charing Cross ("dear queen" from the French *chere reine*), from which all distances in Britain are

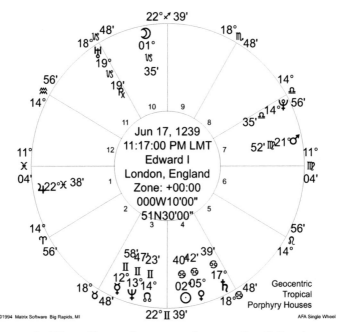

22°✗39'

18°♑48'

☽ 01° ♑ 35'

18°♏48'

14° ♎

35'♎ 14°♆56'

19° ♒ 18°♑
19° ♑
19° ♑℞

56' ♒ 14°

10 | 9

11 | 8

Jun 17, 1239
11:17:00 PM LMT
Edward I
London, England
Zone: +00:00
000W10'00"
51N30'00"

52'♍21°♂

11° ♍ 04'

11° ♓ 04'

♃22°♓38'

12 | 7

1 | 6

2 | 5

3 | 4

14° ♈ 56'

56' ♌ 14°

58'♊7♊23'
♊ ♊ ♊
12° 13°14'
☿ ♆ ☊
18°♉
48'

40'42' 39'
♋ ♋
02°05° 17° ♋
☉ ♀

♄ ♋
48' 18°♋

Geocentric
Tropical
Porphyry Houses

22° ♊ 39'

©1994 Matrix Software Big Rapids, MI | AFA Single Wheel

measured. Edward's mother passed away the following year (Midheaven trine Mercury).

Edward then focused on Scotland. After defeating Scottish King John and forcing him into exile, Edward stole the Stone of Scone and had it placed under a new coronation chair, subsequently used to crown each successive English monarch.

In September 1299, Edward remarried (Midheaven sesquisquare Venus). His bride Margaret, sister of the King of France, was young enough to be his granddaughter (forty-three years his junior). He named his eldest son (later Edward II) Prince of Wales in 1301.

Shortly after Robert the Bruce became King of Scotland, Edward trekked north to combat any reprisals from the Scots. Before he could mount an attack, he died of dysentery at Burgh-on-Sands on July 7, 1307 (progressed Ascendant opposite Sun).

Edward was handsome, tall (6'2.5"), physically impressive, tough, and athletic, a real knight of the first order who inspired confidence in those he ruled. He was brave as a lion (Mars opposite Jupiter and square Midheaven), and a daring strategist. Having the

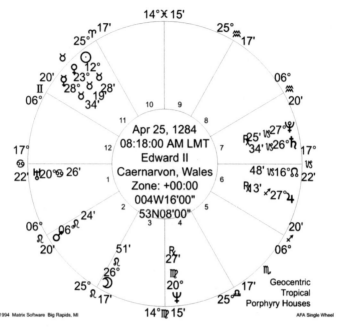

14°♓15'

25°♒17'

♈17'
25°

06°♒
20'

12°
☉
♀♂23°♉
20'
28°♉ ♂19'
♉06° Ⅱ ♂ ♂28'
34'

10 9

11 8

25'♑27°♆
℞34'♑26°♄ 17°
Apr 25, 1284
12 08:18:00 AM LMT 7
Edward II
48'♑16°☊ ♑22°
Caernarvon, Wales
17°♋ 6
22'♅20°♋26' 1
℞3'♐27°♃
Zone: +00:00
2 004W16'00" 5
53N08'00" 3 4

20'♐
06°♐

06°♌
℞27'
20' ♍
♋♌24' 20°♍
06°♌ ♆
51'♌ ♏
26°♌ 17' Geocentric
25°♌ 25°♎ Tropical
☽ Porphyry Houses
17'♌

©1994 Matrix Software Big Rapids, MI 14°♍15' AFA Single Wheel

famed Plantagenet temper, he was a bully or tyrant at times. To some he was an autocrat and to others a man of vision (Mercury and Neptune trine Pluto). His reputation was positive as he ruled with the consent of Parliament and encouraged legal and administrative reforms that forever changed both civil and criminal law. Like most Cancers (especially with the Sun in the fourth house), he sought to make his country secure and safe from its neighbors' interference; he succeeded with Wales but eventually failed with Scotland.

Edward II

In *Nativtas*, Martin Harvey states that Edward II was born at Caernarvon Castle in Wales on April 25, 1284 at 8:21 a.m. LAT (8:18 a.m. LMT). His mother, Eleanor of Castile, died when he was six and a half (progressed Midheaven opposite Neptune, Ascendant conjunct Uranus). Ten years later he became the first Prince of Wales (Midheaven sextile Mercury, Ascendant opposite Saturn). When his father died in 1307 (Midheaven trine Mars), Edward at twenty-three was unprepared to become king and was in many ways the polar opposite of his father. His lover, Piers Gaveston, once exiled by Edward I, returned home as Earl of Cornwall, a title usually reserved for members of the royal family. Edward II had little use for a conventional lifestyle (Uranus rising; Venus rules the fifth house and squares the Moon, ruler of the Ascendant).

For state reasons, in 1308 Edward married Isabella, daughter of the King of France (Midheaven semisquare Venus). Being French, Isabella was quite tolerant of her husband's homosexuality and, like most women of the time, probably thought her French ways could somehow "convert" him. While Isabella and Edward honeymooned in France, Gaveston acted as regent, really rankling the barons who didn't resent the king's choice of paramours as much as they feared an outsider becoming too powerful and thwarting their own selfish interests (early lobbyists?). By 1312, the barons, fed up and on the brink of civil war, kidnapped and beheaded the king's lover (progressed Moon sesquisquare Moon, Ascendant semisquare Neptune).

Five months later a new heir was born. By then, Edward had assumed a new lover—Hugh Despencer—and was rumored to have had relations with Hugh's father as well. Edward's mind was not on warfare in June 1314 as the English Army was crushed by the troops under Robert the Bruce. Hunted by the Scottish king and running for his life, Edward hastily fled home, sad and forlorn (Ascendant conjunct natal Mars and semisquare Neptune). Following eleven years of successive humiliations, Edward finally signed a truce with Robert the Bruce.

In 1325, Isabella, disillusioned by her husband's persistent affairs, fled to France and rebelled against convention by living openly with commoner Roger Mortimer. Intending to become queen in her own right, Isabella (and Roger) plotted a vengeful coup against the government, her husband and the detested Despencers. Isabella garnered considerable support from English barons who wanted Edward removed from power. She assembled an army that landed in Suffolk in October 1326 as Edward and his lovers fled west into Wales. Isabella, the "She Wolf," received much support and soon riots broke out all over southern England.

By the end of November, Isabella was gratified by witnessing the death of Hugh Despencer, whose genitals and bowels were removed and entrails burned before he was beheaded and his remaining body quartered. That October, Hugh's father had suffered a similar fate. Isabella's revenge was almost complete with Edward held prisoner at Berkeley Castle. By the end of January 1327, Edward was forced to abdicate to spare his life. Some who previously accepted Isabella's revenge and excesses began to fear that she and Roger had gone too far and some wanted old, gay Edward back on the throne. After eight months of starvation and humiliation, Edward was brutally murdered on September 22, 1327. In his final agony, Edward had a metal funnel shoved up his rectum and then a red hot poker was thrust inside. The screaming and yelling were piercing to all within earshot but no scar was left on the outside of his body. Edward's progressed Midheaven was square Saturn at his brutal murder, the choice of which was quite fitting at that time for a sodomite.

Like his father, Edward was handsome, tall and blond. With Leo Moon square Venus, he was extravagant and pleasure-seeking but very loyal to his friends (eleventh house planets). His preference for low and base company (today's "rough trade") is shown by Saturn and Pluto in the seventh house trine Venus. Note that the Moon (Ascendant ruler) inconjuncts Saturn (Descendant ruler), strongly indicating the hatred and animosity between Edward and his wife. With Uranus rising, he made little or no attempt to impress anyone; he was simply too unconventional and unpredictable for that historical period. His reign was fraught with deceit, treachery, violence and total incompetence. Like that of King John, Edward II's reign is one most English would prefer to forget.

Edward III

According to a biography by Parke, Edward III was born at Windsor Castle on November 13, 1312 at 5:40 a.m. LAT (5:27 a.m. LMT). *Notable Nativities* by Alan Leo and Martin Harvey's *Nativitas* use a 5:45 a.m. time. Edward was only fourteen when crowned in February 1327 shortly after his father's abdication. While Edward's progressed Midheaven squared Uranus, his father was brutally murdered by his mother and her lover. A year later, to escape his mother's control, Edward married Philippa of Hainault (Midheaven opposite Pluto). With his father's demise, Edward began plotting against his mother and her lover Roger Mortimer.

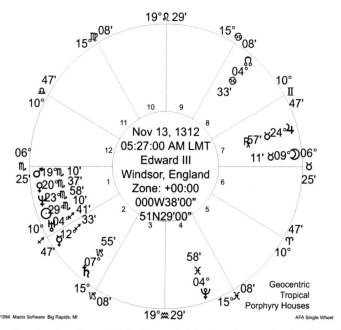

Chart data:

19° ♌ 29'

15 ♍ 08'

15° ♋ 08'

04° ♋ 33' ☊

10° ♊ 47'

47' ♎ 10°

10 9

11 8

Nov 13, 1312
05:27:00 AM LMT
Edward III
Windsor, England
Zone: +00:00
000W38'00"
51N29'00"

12 7

1 6

2 5

3 4

57' ♇ 24° ♃

11' ♅ 09° ☽ 06° ♉ 25'

06° ♏ 25'

♂ 19 ♏ 10'
♀ 20 ♏ 37'
♄ 23 ♏ 58' (⊕)
29 ♏ 41'
⊕ 04 ♐ 33'
♆ 12 ♐

10° ♐ 47'

07° ♑
♄

55'
♑ ☊

58'
♓ 04°
♆

47' ♈ 10°

15° ♑ 08'

19° ♒ 29'

15° ♓ 08'

Geocentric
Tropical
Porphyry Houses

AFA Single Wheel

Finally, in October 1330, he and his henchmen broke into his mother's bedchamber, arrested Roger Mortimer and sent him to the Tower of London for execution. He banished his mother to Castle Rising in Norfolk, where she stayed the remainder of her life (Midheaven trine Saturn, Ascendant conjunct Mars). Edward was at last firmly secure on the throne.

When his maternal uncle, the King of France, died in 1328, Edward claimed the French throne. For the next decade, he wavered between releasing his claim and waging war. When the French king confiscated Edward's Duchy of Gascony in 1337, Edward declared war on France (Ascendant conjunct Neptune opposite Jupiter). The first major battle of what came to be known as the Hundred Years War was at sea near Sluys in Flanders in the summer of 1340. English casualties were 4,000 while France's were 25,000. During the Battle of Crecy six years later, the English lost 800 while the French lost 30,000.

The year 1348 was mixed for Edward. He founded the Order of the Garter in late June and two months later the Black Death claimed his daughter. Before the plague was over, nearly one-quarter of the European population was destroyed. In 1358, Edward was finally freed from his mother by her death (Midheaven square Saturn) and he buried her next to Mortimer.

Edward's eldest son, also called Edward the ``Black Prince'' (born June 15, 1330), caused quite a stir at court by marrying Countess Joan of Kent, once reputed to be the king's mistress. In 1369, Philippa died (Midheaven semisquare Uranus sesquisquare Pluto) and Edward went into decline and senility. He wasn't lonely long as Philippa's lady-in-waiting, Alice Perrers, moved into the royal chambers. Being unsound, Edward gave Alice Philippa's jewels and before long was unduly influenced by her at court. Alice was greedy and shameless to the end when she stole rings off the king's fingers when he died on June 21, 1377. Some rumored that Edward died from syphilis caught from Alice, though that disease probably didn't invade Europe until after Columbus' New World voyages. Some accused Alice of witchcraft in turning the king's eyes away from affairs of state (Midheaven inconjunct Jupiter).

Edward was a great soldier, a strong leader and self-confident (stellium in Scorpio in the first house). He led a lavish and luxuriant life—a Taurus Moon sextile Pluto doesn't hold down expenditures. Despite the strong Scorpionic exterior, Edward was a calm and resourceful man with considerable vigor (rising Mars conjunct Venus). Always chivalrous and honorable (Jupiter opposite Neptune), he managed to embroil England in a series of wars that would prohibit peace on English shores until the death of Richard III more than a century later.

Richard II

Born in Bordeaux, France on January 6, 1367 at 10:00 a.m. LAT (10:10 a.m. LMT), according to Martin Harvey, Richard lost his father (the Black Prince) at age nine (progressed Ascendant sesquisquare Saturn) and his grandfather (Edward III) at age ten (Midheaven conjunct Mercury, Ascendant opposite Mars). In the spring of 1381, Wat Tyler led a peasant revolt against payment of a poll tax. Though only 14, Richard met the revolters face-to-face and negotiated with their leader. The revolt was squelched with the murder of Tyler and the people were impressed by young Richard's bravery (Midheaven semisquare Saturn). In January 1382, Richard

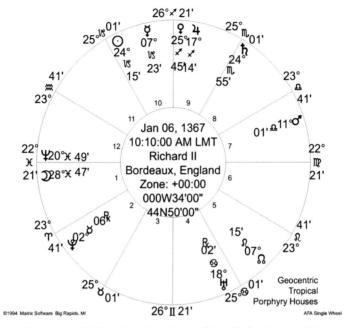

Chart details:

26°♐21'
25°♑ 01'
☉ 24° ☿ 07' ♀ ♃ 25°17' 25° ♏ 01'
♑ 15' ♑ 23' ♐ ♐ 4514' ♄ 24° ♏ 55' 23° ♎ 41'
41' ♒ 23°
10   9   8
11   01' ♎ 11° ♂
22° ♓ Ψ20°♓49'   12   Jan 06, 1367   7   22° ♍ 21'
21' ☽28°♓47'   1   10:10:00 AM LMT
                        Richard II
                        Bordeaux, England
                        Zone: +00:00   6
                        000W34'00"
                        44N50'00"   5
23° ♈ 06' ♅   2   3   4
41' ♇02° ♆   15'
                        ☽02'   ♌07° ☋   41' ♌ 23°
                        ♋
                        18°
25° ♉ 01'   ♅   01'   Geocentric
                        25° ♋   Tropical
                        Porphyry Houses

©1994 Matrix Software Big Rapids, MI   26° ♊ 21'   AFA Single Wheel

married Anne of Bohemia, daughter of the Holy Roman Emperor (Midheaven square Mars) and from all accounts it was a happy though barren union.

Richard reached majority in 1387 with trouble brewing over Robert de Vere's influence on him. With the threat of war, de Vere was exiled and Richard overthrew the council two years later (Midheaven opposite Uranus). When Anne died of the plague in 1394 (Midheaven sextile Saturn conjunct Sun), Richard went mad and became a dictatorial tyrant, taking revenge on the barons who had humiliated him nine years earlier.

In November 1396, Richard married Isabella of Valois, twenty years his junior and daughter of the King of France. This arranged union secured the peace between these warring nations (Ascendant sextile Uranus). The following year, Richard exiled three of the Lords Appellants (Ascendant sextile Neptune) and a year later Henry Bolingbroke, the Duke of Lancaster (Midheaven sextile Moon). The future Henry IV did not take this lying down. In February 1399 the Lancaster Estates were confiscated and seized (Ascendant sesquisquare Mercury) after the death of Richard's uncle,

John of Gaunt. Henry landed in August and the following month Richard was deposed by Parliament. Refusing to abdicate, Richard was banished to the Tower of London and then to Pontefract Castle, where he died between February 9 and 17, 1400, probably by orders of his cousin Henry IV (Ascendant opposite Saturn).

Richard was a mass of contradictions (Neptune rising trine Uranus). A weak and unbalanced man (Sun opposite Uranus), capricious and prodigal, his perversity caused considerable consternation at court. Very handsome, almost effeminate in appearance (Pisces Moon on the Ascendant), his demeanor when young was delicate and fragile. More interested in the arts than in military matters (Venus on the Midheaven), his reputation suffered because of his unjust treatment of those he perceived as his enemies. He was far too trusting and naive politically and he left the affairs of state to his advisors. Detractors called him cowardly but proud, extravagant and temperamental. With his death, battles for control of the English throne between descendants of Edward III erupted over the next 85 years and culminated in the War of the Roses.

The House of Lancaster

Henry IV

Henry IV, son of John of Gaunt and Blanche of Lancaster, was born in Spilsby, England at Bolingbroke Castle on April 4, 1366 (O.S.) at noon LAT (12:01 p.m. LMT) according to *Nativitas* by Martin Harvey. There is some dispute as to both the date and the year. Most reference books give the date as April 3, 1367, according to *American Astrology* magazine (data source unverified).

Henry's mother died when he was three (progressed Ascendant square Saturn) and at the tender age of fourteen, in 1390, Henry married Mary de Bohun (Ascendant trine Mars). In 1392 Henry went off on a crusade to the Holy Land but never got there, being detained in Lithuania. Two years later his wife died (Midheaven opposite Jupiter-Saturn). The tumultuous year of 1399 began with the death of his father, the Duke of Lancaster or John of Gaunt (Midheaven opposite Jupiter, Ascendant trine Pluto). Soon after, King Richard II confiscated the Lancaster estates, taking away Henry's inheritance. An army was put together so Henry could reclaim his birthright and in August 1399 Henry arrived from exile in France. At the end of September, Parliament deposed Richard and Henry was proclaimed king. His right to occupy the throne was somewhat dubious as he was descended from the fourth son of Edward III and others had a better claim to the throne. thus did Henry

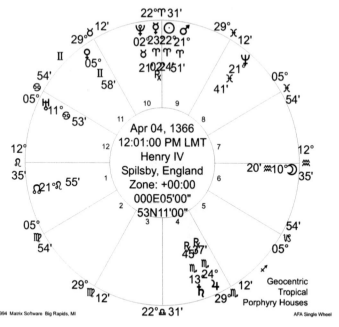

Geocentric
Tropical
Porphyry Houses

Apr 04, 1366
12:01:00 PM LMT
Henry IV
Spilsby, England
Zone: +00:00
000E05'00"
53N11'00"

become known as the "Usurper." Since Richard was still alive, Henry couldn't be secure until he had the old king done away with, a *fait accompli* by the end of February of the next year.

In 1403 Henry married Joanna, daughter of the King of Navarre. She had previously been married to the Duke of Brittany who was many years her senior. Her union with Henry was one of convenience and they had no offspring (Midheaven semisquare Uranus, Ascendant square Venus). Six years after Henry's death, Joanna was falsely accused of practicing witchcraft, more likely than not to confiscate her vast estates. Henry's brief reign was marked by one war after another, both internal and on the continent. He developed a skin rash (some say it was leprosy) and died on March 20, 1413 (Midheaven conjunct Venus semisquare Sun, Mercury, Mars). He died in the Jerusalem Chamber at Westminster Abbey, his kingdom nonetheless united. He was a short and stocky man whose temperament and personality made him unpopular, only partly due to his usurpation of the throne. He was the first king to speak English as a native, all his predecessors preferring French.

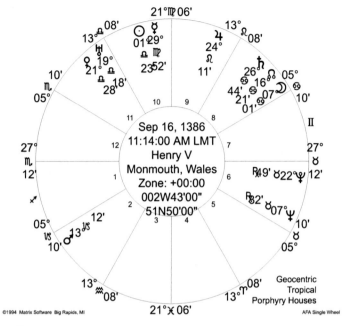

21°♍06'

13°⚷08'

13°⚷ 01°⚷29° ☉☿
19° ♎ ♍
21° ♎ 23°52'
28°18'

13°♌08'

24° ♃
♌
11'

26°♌ 05° ♄
44'16°♋ ☽♋
21°07'♋ 10'
01'

10

9

11

8

II

Sep 16, 1386
11:14:00 AM LMT
Henry V
Monmouth, Wales
Zone: +00:00
002W43'00"
51N50'00"

27°
♏
12'

12

7

27°
♉

1

6

℞49' ♉22° ♅ 12'

2

5

℞32' ♉07' ♆ 10'
♉

05°
♑
10'

♂13°♑ 12'

3

4

♉
05°

13°♒08'

13°♈08'

21°♓06'

Geocentric
Tropical
Porphyry Houses

©1994 Matrix Software Big Rapids, MI

AFA Single Wheel

Henry V

Henry of Monmouth was born September 16, 1386 (O.S.) at 11:22 a.m. LAT (11:14 a.m. LMT) in Monmouth Castle in Wales (source: fifteenth century chart given in a Latin manuscript with a 29 Scorpio Ascendant). His mother, Mary de Bohun, died when he was eight (Midheaven conjunct Mercury), five years before his father, Henry Bolingbroke, usurped the throne from his cousin Richard II in 1399 (Ascendant semisquare Venus inconjunct Moon). Henry's youth was wild and riotous and he quarreled constantly with his father during his reign.

Becoming king in his own right in 1413 (Midheaven square Mars-Uranus), Henry renewed the war for the French crown begun by his great-grandfather Edward III. Henry's victory at Agincourt was overwhelming: 8,000 English soldiers fought 50,000 Frenchmen, but due to rain-dampened ground, the French (who had fought on horseback) sank into the mire because their armor was too heavy and cumbersome. The English clearly had the advantage because they fought on foot and used the longbow (Midheaven conjunct

Uranus). Over the next four years, Henry's campaigns in Normandy resulted in one victory after another. But all this warfare was bankrupting him, so he had his stepmother, Joan of Navarre, arrested and falsely accused of witchcraft, thus confiscating her state dowry and properties.

Henry finally decided to marry. His bride, Catherine of Valois (born October 27, 1401—source: Harvey quoted Latin records for 9:50 a.m. sundial or LAT, 9:34 GMT). She was the French king's sister. Because the dauphin was retarded, he was disinherited and Henry V became the heir to the French throne upon his marriage in June 1420 (Midheaven sextile Jupiter, Ascendant sextile Venus). But their union was short lived as Henry died of dysentery on August 31, 1422 at Vincennes (Midheaven square Saturn, Ascendant inconjunct Pluto), leaving the throne to his eight-and-a-half-month-old son Henry VI.

Henry was one of the most enigmatic persons to ever sit on the English throne. The personification of a Scorpio Ascendant with a Virgo Midheaven, he was sober and moral with a distinctly pious demeanor and was also very stern. He had an athletic build and was very handsome in a swashbuckling sort of way; he loved adventure due to Mars semisquare the Ascendant. Saturn trine the Ascendant, however, made him humorless and merciless in punishing his enemies, yet scrupulous in seeing that justice always prevailed due to Sun in Libra. He looked more like a monk than a warrior and he had a religious side that made him chaste and meditative due to Jupiter sitting in the ninth house square the Ascendant.

Henry VI

Henry VI was born in Windsor Castle, London on December 6, 1421 at 4:00 p.m. LAT, 3:56 LMT (source: Harvey quoted records in Latin) and became king less than nine months later upon the premature death of his father (progressed Ascendant conjunct Pluto). With the death of his grandfather, the King of France, he also ruled France before he was a year old. The regency was left in the hands of his two uncles who constantly squabbled over control of the young king. Meanwhile, his mother Catherine had married Owen Tudor, grandfather of Henry VII, who would later usurp the throne from Richard III. Henry was crowned King of England in Novem-

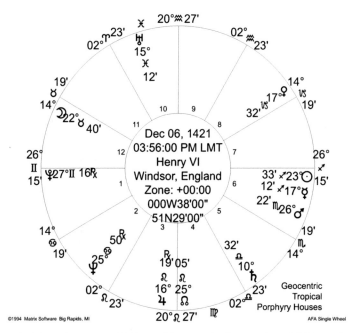

Dec 06, 1421
03:56:00 PM LMT
Henry VI
Windsor, England
Zone: +00:00
000W38'00"
51N29'00"

©1994 Matrix Software Big Rapids, MI

Geocentric
Tropical
Porphyry Houses

AFA Single Wheel

ber 1429 and crowned King of France in December 1431 at Notre Dame. His mother died in January 1437 (Ascendant square Saturn), paving the way for Henry to exercise his right to rule rather than reign, no longer responsible to his council, which had been quite ineffective in running the country.

In April 1445, Henry married Margaret of Anjou (born March 23, 1430), daughter of the King of Sicily. She was a scheming, stern and ruthless woman, imbued with vindictiveness and determined that her husband should prevail over anyone who would brook his authority. As they had no children for the fist eight years of their marriage, the heir was Edward IV. When Henry was married, his Midheaven was conjunct Uranus and the Ascendant opposite Venus. In many respects, Margaret should have been queen in her own right for she was more effective politically and militarily than her husband—she was an Aries, a warrior at heart and a good one to boot.

In August 1453, Henry went mad and fell into a catatonic state, leaving the kingdom under the protectorship of the Duke of York (progressed Sun opposite Neptune, Midheaven square sun). Henry didn't even realize he had fathered a son. Due to conflicts between the Duke of York and Queen Margaret, York took up arms at St. Albans in May 1455, making Henry a virtual pawn at the hands of this ambitious man. Needless to say, Margaret didn't take this lying down and thus began the War of the Roses (Ascendant sextile Moon inconjunct Sun). Margaret was fighting to keep her husband on the throne and finally defeated York in 1459, a victory that was reversed the following year. Henry was forced to disinherit his son in favor of York and his offspring (Midheaven sesquisquare Jupiter, Ascendant conjunct Neptune trine Mars). York was killed in battle in late 1460 and his son Edward IV took steps to take over. Henry was deposed by Edward in March 1461 and fled to Scotland. Margaret fled to France to seek safety from her cousin, the King of France. Henry was captured in July 1465 and held in the Tower of London (Ascendant sesquisquare Uranus), regaining the throne briefly from October 1470 to May 1471 (Midheaven opposite Saturn sesquisquare Mars). Margaret was seized at Tewksbury in May 1471, thus sealing Henry's fate. Henry was murdered on orders from Edward IV on May 24, 1741 at about 11:30 p.m., thus ending the Lancastrian dynasty.

Like many Sagittarians, Henry was gentle and honest to the extreme, a pious man who dressed simply and looked more like a monk than a king. A sensitive, weak and other-worldly individual (Sun inconjunct Neptune), he lacked the ruthlessness to run a kingdom and had little, if any, political skill or military prowess. One might say he would have preferred never to have become king at all, for he let things slide and was overly well-meaning and trusting. His ineptitude provoked a war that was to practically ruin England over the next three decades. In the end, both sides lost.

The House of York

Edward IV

Edward IV was born in Rouen, France on April 28, 1442 at 2:00 a.m. LAT, 1:56 a.m. LMT (source: Harvey says there's some confusion about he date, but it seems accurate and valid from Latin research). He was the son of Richard, Duke of York (born September 21, 1411) and Cicely Neville (born May 3, 1415). His father was proclaimed the next King of England in November 1460 but two months later he died in battle at Wakefield along with his son Edmund (Midheaven trine Venus, Ascendant sextile Saturn). Edward staked his claim to be king in March the following year after the battle of Towton and was crowned at the end of June 1461, thus founding a new dynasty. With the old king and queen on the run, Edwards's position was not all that secure; but, due to the Machiavellian tactics of the Earl of Warwick (known as the "Kingmaker"), he managed to keep his power intact.

In May 1464, Edward secretly married Elizabeth Woodville, a commoner and widow five year his senior. They met in a forest where she had gone to ask Edward to restore her husband's land. Edward made a play for her but she rebuffed him by telling him that if he wanted her he would have to propose. She wasn't content to be just a king's mistress. Soon after their wedding, her large family arrived at court *en masse* and Edward passed out favors and titles ga-

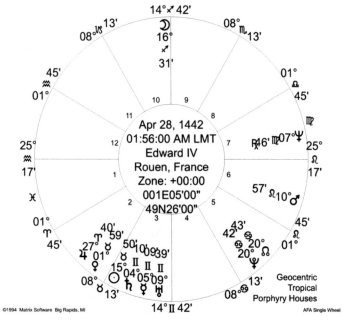

14°✕42'

08°♑13'   ☽16°✕31'   08°♏13'

45'   ♒   01°

25°♒17'   Apr 28, 1442
01:56:00 AM LMT
Edward IV
Rouen, France
Zone: +00:00
001E05'00"
49N26'00"   01°♎45'

℞46'♏07°♇   25°♌17'

57'♌10°♂

♓   01°♈45'

40'59'   ♈27°♉
♀01°   50'♉10°♋39'

15°04°♊   ♊   ♊
08°♉13'   ☉   ♄♀♅05°09°

43'42'♋   ♋20°♌20°   45'
♇   01°♌   45'

08°♋   13'   Geocentric
Tropical
Porphyry Houses

©1994 Matrix Software Big Rapids, MI   14°♊42'   AFA Single Wheel

lore, thus enraging the nobility. Her five brothers and seven sisters were all raised to high rank and married into moneyed families. Their influence on Edward was conspicuous and alarmed men like Warwick who saw his power and influence over the king wasting away.

Warwick switched sides against the king,, who was forced to flee to Burgundy to save his life. It seems that Warwick had made peace with Queen Margaret and was now conspiring to place her husband back on the throne. Henry left the Tower of London in October 1470, retaking the throne Edward had taken form him nine years earlier. But after the battle of Barnet in April 1471, Warwick lay dead; one month later Margaret was trounced at Tewksbury and Edward again seized the crown. Henry was murdered on orders from Edward at the end of May 1471 (Ascendant conjunct Jupiter), making Edward's position now more secure than ever.

Trouble began brewing six years later due to the strong ambitions of his brother George, the Duke of Clarence. Clarence had turned traitor a decade earlier when he sided with Warwick against the king, but Edward had forgiven his brother when he retook the throne. Edward was afraid that if Clarence went through with his impending marriage to Mary of Burgundy, he would invade England and take over. Finally, after his brother kept haranguing him and embarrassing him in public, he sent him to the Tower and had him drowned in a vat of wine in February 1478 (Midheaven sesquisquare Saturn). Edward could breathe a bit easier as well after 1482 when old Queen Margaret died in France. But victory wouldn't last long because Edward became mysteriously ill in March 1483 and died two weeks later on April 9, 1483 (Midheaven sesquisquare Uranus, Ascendant sextile Pluto).

Edward was the exact opposite of King Henry VI. Tall and handsome, he was an affable and approachable individual who loved to be at the center of things (Moon at the Midheaven). Edward also had an eye for the ladies and was always seen in the latest fashions. His Sagittarius Midheaven gave his court the reputation of being self-indulgent and extravagant with food and wine flowing to abundance. But that Aquarian Ascendant made him egalitarian and somewhat lazy with a tendency toward corpulence in later years. Some said Edward had the morals of an alley cat and was greedy and power hungry. He seemed to be more interested in people than in politics. He was vain to the extreme, but paid little attention to the enmity his marriage caused due to the Neptune in the seventh house square three planets in Gemini.

Edward V

Edward V was born in London on November 2, 1470 at 4:06 p.m. according to contemporary astrologer John Argentine, as shown in *Born to Reign* by Nicholas Campion. I've rectified the chart to 4:00 p.m. LAT, 3:46 p.m. LMT. Over the years, family squabbles became a part of his youth and he was deeply affected by the assassination of his uncle, the Duke of Clarence, in 1478 (progressed Midheaven square Uranus semisquare Moon). Edward became king at age twelve upon the untimely death of his father (progressed Midheaven trine Jupiter sesquisquare Pluto). Many at court feared another minority government under the rulership of the detested Woodville family so they suggested that a Lord Protector be appointed. Their selection was Richard, Duke of Gloucester, Edwards's uncle (Richard III). Bad choice: It seems jealous relatives

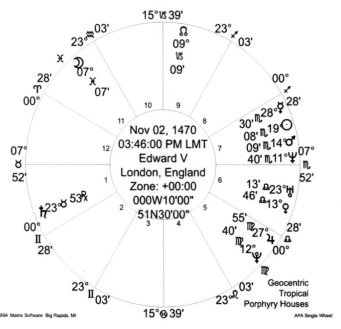

15°♑39'

23°♒03'   ☊ 09° ♑ 09°   23°♐ 03'

♓   ♃ 07°♓ 07'

28' ♈ 00°   07'   00°♐   ☿ 28'

10   9

11   8   30'♏28'   08'♏19 ☉

07°♉ 52'   12   Nov 02, 1470   03:46:00 PM LMT   Edward V   London, England   Zone: +00:00   000W10'00"   51N30'00"   09'♏14 ♂   40'♏11°Ψ   07°♏ 52'

1   7   6

♄23°♉ 53'℞   2   13'♎23°♅   46'♎13°♀

00° ♊ 28'   3   4   55'♍40' ♍27° ♃   28'♎   ♍12° ⚷   00°

♍

23°♊ 03'   03'♌   23°♌   Geocentric   Tropical   Porphyry Houses

©1994 Matrix Software Big Rapids, MI   15°♋39'   AFA Single Wheel

fought over the young king (Moon-Pluto opposition, Sun-Saturn opposition).

Edward's mother, Elizabeth Woodville, left Ludlow Castle, heading for London with her two sons, on April 24, 1483. Six days later his uncle and lord protector kidnaped young Edward, took him to London and put him in the Tower of London for "safekeeping." The queen and her other son took sanctuary in Westminster Abbey, but after a while Richard managed to coax the queen into giving up her other son, who was then placed with his brother in the Tower. The princes were last seen alive on June 16, 1483 and were more than likely murdered shortly before their uncle, Richard III, was crowned on July 6. A conspiracy erupted to rescue the princes a month later, but Richard squelched it. If they were still alive at the time, there would have been no need to quell the revolt, would there?

Richard had the two princes declared bastards due to his brother's (Edward IV) marriage contract with Lady Butler prior to his marriage with Elizabeth Woodville; his brother's marriage was invalid. In 1672, workmen in the Tower of London found skeletons of two young boys under a flight of stone steps—presumably the remains of Edward V and his brother. Exactly what occurred to Edward V during that tempestuous time in his life (progressed Ascendant opposite Mercury sesquisquare Venus) is pure speculation and the part Richard III might have played in his disappearance is still under investigation by historians.

Richard III

Richard was born in Fotheringay Castle on October 2, 1452, the son of Richard, Duke of York, and Cicely Neville. Martin Harvey prefers the birth time of 9:15 a.m., which I have adjusted slightly because I feel a later time more clearly describes the life of this man who has been so vilified. Thus the time has been rectified by me to 9:35 a.m. LAT (9:22 a.m. LMT). (Source: Harvey said 9:15 a.m. time deduced from 1452 account in Latin, time speculative.) At first I didn't want to believe that Richard had Scorpio rising, its negative impact seeming to be more propaganda than historical fact. But after weeks of thorough investigation, I had to agree that many traits and characteristics attributed to Richard could only be

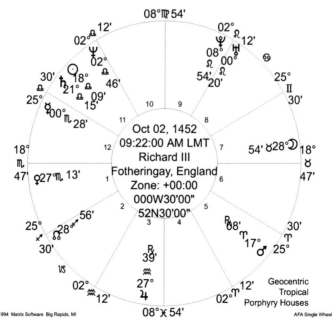

Oct 02, 1452
09:22:00 AM LMT
Richard III
Fotheringay, England
Zone: +00:00
000W30'00"
52N30'00"

Geocentric
Tropical
Porphyry Houses

©1994 Matrix Software Big Rapids, MI

AFA Single Wheel

accounted for by placing the dreaded sign of the serpent or scorpion on the Ascendant.

Richard was sent abroad for safekeeping at age eight in the early days of the War of the Roses. His father was promised the throne of England in October 1460, but two months later lay dead on the battlefield at Wakefield (progressed Midheaven inconjunct Mars). A few months later, Richard's eldest brother, Edward IV, became king (progressed Sun trine Jupiter in the third house). Richard's sudden elevation in status is shown by Uranus crossing his Midheaven; he was made Duke of Gloucester by his brother later that year. After Edward IV murdered Henry VI in the spring of 1471, Richard's power increased (progressed Midheaven sextile Venus, Ascendant trine Uranus) with Pluto crossing his natal Midheaven.

Richard married his second cousin, Anne Neville (born June 11, 1456), whose former husband had been Prince Edward (son of Henry VI) and whose father was the Earl of Warwick, the "Kingmaker" and the most powerful man in England during the previous decade. Richard received many of Warwick's honors and land prior to his union with Anne (progressed Midheaven trine Moon, Ascendant sextile Neptune). Richard's brother George, Duke of Clarence, was married to Anne's sister Isabel. It seems that Clarence wanted all the land and honors for himself and hid Anne from Richard in a church. To marry Anne Neville, Richard had to agree to give up some of the estate to Clarence. Note the Moon in the seventh house in Taurus opposing Venus (ruler of the seventh house) and both square Jupiter, ruler of Richard's second house of income and assets. At the time of his marriage, transiting Jupiter was trine its own position in late Libra conjunct Uranus, and transiting Saturn was square his Ascendant. Richard's job during his brother's "second term in office" was to guard the northern border with Scotland from foreign invasion. The murder of Clarence, regardless of their former differences, weighed heavily on Richard's shoulders in early 1478 (progressed Ascendant semisquare Saturn). Uranus and Neptune were conjunct at 28 Scorpio, opposing his Moon and square his Jupiter in the third house of siblings.

When Edward IV died in April 1483, Richard's life turned upside down. His progressed Midheaven was now sextile Pluto and the progressed Ascendant was trine the same planet. Richard's progressed Sun was sitting on his natal Ascendant, and the progressed Moon at thirteen degrees Cancer aspecting his Moon, Venus and Jupiter. What occurred over the three months from April 9 to July 6 is a source of speculation. It's known he kidnaped young Edward V and took him to the Tower of London and soon after begged the queen to part with her other son as well. It's known the two princes were last seen alive in the middle of June, some two and a half weeks before Richard's coronation, but before Parliament had asked him to become king. Whether Richard directly ordered the murder of the boys or whether someone loyal to Richard did the dirty deed may never be known. Due to rumors circulating at the time, there wasn't much that Richard could have done to correct the situation: He was in a no-win position.

In April 1484, Richard's son died, making his position on the throne quite precarious (progressed Moon at 28 Cancer). A year later, in March 1485, his wife Anne died of tuberculosis as Jupiter squared his Midheaven and Uranus was inconjunct his Moon. Some believed that Richard got rid of his wife to marry his niece Elizabeth, the prospective bride of Henry Tudor. None of this can be proven (Richard had Mercury in the twelfth house square Uranus, so rumors were everywhere), but Henry Tudor saw it as a chance to grab the throne and formed an army to oust Richard. Henry landed in early August 1485 with 2,000 men loaned by the King of France. Marching through Wales on his way to meet Richard at Bosworth, he picked up support, doubling his troops. The battle of Bosworth was short. Richard's horse was shot out from under him, his crown flew into the bushes, he was cut down, his naked corpse was thrown across a horse and his troops were taken to Leicester. Henry Tudor picked up the crown and placed it on his head, thus ending the Plantagenet dynasty that had ruled England for 331 years. The War of the Roses also ceased. Henry Tudor's reign marked the end of the Middle Ages in England.

Richard's progressed Midheaven at the time of his death was semisquare Venus, ruler of his seventh house of open enemies as well as the twelfth house of self-undoing. His Midheaven was also sesquisquare natal Jupiter and within orb of opposing progressed Mars, which had been in retrograde motion since his birth. The progressed Ascendant was ironically trine that same progressed Mars (not that it did him any good), but was still within orb of a semisquare to his progressed Saturn. Richard's progressed Moon at 17 Leo 30 was semisquare his natal Neptune, so the ruler of his eighth house was in affliction to the ruler of his fourth house. Transiting Jupiter was semisquare his Sun and transiting Saturn was conjunct his progressed Venus; thus, he couldn't win over his enemies. At best, Richard might have held on for another year as transiting Pluto was approaching a conjunction with his Sun.

Richard's life was the source of so much propaganda and smear tactics that it's difficult to separate fact from fiction. It's known that his birth was long and arduous. Not only was his mother thirty-seven at the time, but more than likely he was a breach birth. Thus began the implication he was somehow deformed from birth. It's known one of his shoulders was higher than the other, but contemporary sources make no mention of him being a hunchback. One must consider his temperament and actions relative to the time in which he lived. After all, this was the age of Machiavelli and people weren't always nice to each other. His reign took place during a turbulent period in English history, what with the usurpations of his brother Edward and the murder of Henry VI, not to mention the princes. Sun conjunct Saturn does make one overly ambitious and inclined to be secretive and reserved. Unlike his brother, who was a bon vivant and libertine, Richard was a prude, completely faithful to his wife and never derelict in his duty.

Richard was always a loyal brother as shown by the Sun conjunct Saturn in the eleventh house, and was overly generous to his friends due to Sun-Saturn trine Jupiter. His reputation as an able administrator in the north of England has been overshadowed by the nefarious activities that took place during his reign. Scorpio rising does indicate a tendency toward ruthlessness, especially on the battlefield where the Sun-Mars opposition came into play. The trouble in his life seems to come from the T-square involving the Moon, Venus and Jupiter and the rulers of the third, seventh and eighth houses.

In the end, if Richard had been more open and candid, he might not have gone down in history as such a nasty guy. He was a bad judge of character until it was too late. Most of his friends were those from childhood and he was overwhelmed at the intrigue so prevalent at court. In one context, his entire reign was simply protecting his family's fortunes from interference from those he considered usurpers. I can't buy the cruelty and cynicism portrayed by Shakespeare and early biographers. Richard was a man of his times, protecting his interests as best he saw fit. The fifteenth century was a time of one usurpation after another, first with Henry IV, then Edward IV, and finally Richard III. And we shouldn't forget that Richard's successor also took the throne by force, so maybe Henry VII isn't as blameless as history has presumed him to be.

The Tudors

Henry VII

Henry Tudor was born at Pembroke Castle, Wales on January 28, 1457 at 3:00 a.m. LAT (3:15 a.m. LMT) according to *Nativitas* by Martin Harvey. He was the son of Edmund Tudor, who had died three months prior, and Margaret Beauford, a young girl four months shy of her fourteenth birthday (born May 31, 1443). Henry's family tree was connected to John of Gaunt, third son of Edward III, from both his first and third wives. Henry's grandfather was Owen Tudor, second husband to Catherine de Valois, widow of Henry V. Henry VII spent his youth in Wales until the summer of 1471 when he fled to France and lived for the next fourteen years (progressed Midheaven inconjunct Moon square Jupiter, Ascendant sextile Sun trine Uranus).

Accepted as heir to the House of Lancaster, though descended from a female line, he was relatively unknown in England when he landed at Milford Haven to claim his inheritance. The death of Richard III's wife in the spring of 1485 made it clear that the Yorkists had no apparent living heirs except Henry's cousin Elizabeth, to whom he had been betrothed for more than a year. Gathering support form Wales to Bosworth, Henry Tudor trounced Richard III, picking up the crown from the ground and placing it on his head. The date was August 22, 1485, a memorable date in Eng-

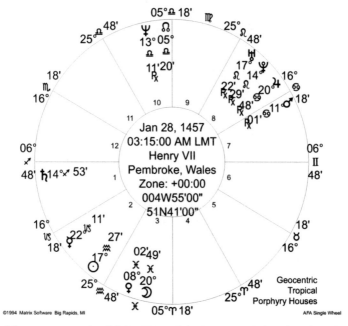

05°♎18' ♍

25°♏48'   ♅ ♌ 25°♌48'
                13°05°
                ♎ ♎
              11'20'
                  ♇

18'   17°♌ ♆ 16°
♏   14°♆
16°   22'♌ 20°♃ ♋
                    29' ♋ 18'
        10   9   48'♋ ♋ 01'♋11'♂18'
    11   ♋

06°   12   Jan 28, 1457   7   06°
♐   03:15:00 AM LMT   ♊
48' ♄14°♐ 53' 1   Henry VII   6   48'
                Pembroke, Wales
            2   Zone: +00:00
                004W55'00"   5
16°   51N41'00"
♑   11'   3   4   18'
18' ♑ ♀22°♑ 27'   ♉
        17°   02'49'   16°
        ⊙ ♒   ♓ ♓
25°   08°20°
♒48'   ♀ ☽   25°♈48' Geocentric
            ♓ 05°♈18'   Tropical
©1994 Matrix Software Big Rapids, MI   Porphyry Houses
                                    AFA Single Wheel

lish history. Not only did the War of the Roses end that day, but also the Middle Ages and feudalism gasped their last breath. England could now enter a new age under the Tudors. (Henry's progressed Ascendant was sesquisquare Pluto and his progressed Sun was sitting at the midpoint of Moon and Venus.) Five months later, Henry lived up to his betrothal promise and married Elizabeth of York (born February 11, 1466), daughter of Edward IV and sister to the deposed Edward V whom her uncle Richard III had locked in the Tower of London. Talk about a dysfunctional family! To learn what Elizabeth looked like, view a standard deck of cards: She was the model for the queen.

Despite theirs being an arranged union of the Red Rose and White Rose, Henry and Elizabeth managed to marry their children off to thwart further foreign conflicts, which they both felt England could ill afford. Arthur was married to Catherine of Aragon, daughter of Ferdinand and Isabela of Spain; Mary was married to the King of France; and Margaret to the King of Scotland.

Five years after Columbus sailed for the New World, England backed an expedition under John Cabot's helm (progressed

Midheaven square Pluto). Henry's personal life took a turn for the worse when his son Arthur, the Prince of Wales, died in April 1502 of consumption (Midheaven trine Moon and Jupiter). The next year Prince Henry, now heir to the throne, said he would marry his brother's widow after receiving a dispensation from the Pope. In February 1503, Queen Elizabeth died of an infection from her last childbirth (Ascendant square Neptune inconjunct Pluto). Henry was devastated and suffered serious depressions. His health failed and by 1507 he developed tuberculosis. He passed away on April 12, 1509 (Midheaven sesquisquare Mars, Ascendant conjunct Mercury).

Henry was tall, with a dark complexion, blue eyes and a gaunt frame. He appeared frail and had bad teeth, all typical of Saturn rising. Henry was a penny pincher and miser who personally audited royal accounts and left his country with a full treasury for the first time in a century. Note that Saturn trines Uranus, ruler of his Sun sign, which is also conjunct Pluto, ruler of the twelfth house of what came before Henry sat on the throne. Henry's interest in foreign trade is shown by the Sun (ruler of the ninth house) in the second house and in aspect to the outer planets. Henry was always cautious and prudent, seldom wasting a cent. His detached demeanor seldom invited confidences and despite his strong gifts, he was not a very popular monarch. His wise and firm reign left England in a much stronger position than ever before. He would have made a good chairman of the board for he was astute and capable. Always cool headed, unemotional and moderate, his reign is remembered as the exact opposite of that of his son.

Henry VIII

Henry VIII was born at Greenwich Palace on June 28, 1491 at 8:45 a.m. sundial time, according to *Nativitas* by Martin Harvey. After working with this chart, I found it to be thirty-five minutes early, so the chart here is the rectified one calculated for 9:20 a.m. LAT (9:24 a.m. LMT).

Henry was an active, yet quite studious individual during his childhood. He was a highly cultured intellect of sorts with an eye for the ladies and the good life. With the death of his brother Arthur in 1502 (progressed Ascendant sesquisquare Saturn), Henry, as

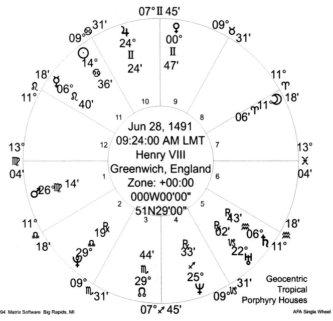

07°♊45'

09♋31'

4°♋14'
☉

18'
11°♌

ν06°♌40'

09°♉31'

4 24°♊24'
♃

♀ 00°♊47'

11°♈18'
☽ 11°♈
06'♈

13°♍04'
♂26°♍14'

13°♓04'

11°♎18'
ψ29°♎

18'♒
♄06°♒11'
♅22°♑
02'♑

10
9
8
7
6
5

11
12
1
2
3
4

Jun 28, 1491
09:24:00 AM LMT
Henry VIII
Greenwich, England
Zone: +00:00
000W00'00"
51N29'00"

19♐
29°♏31'
44'♏
09°♏
33'
25°♐
ψ
43'
♄

Geocentric
Tropical
Porphyry Houses

09°♑31'

©1994 Matrix Software Big Rapids, MI

AFA Single Wheel

07°♐45'

Prince of Wales, had to settle down somewhat and assume a more serious mood. A few months following the death of his mother in 1503 (Ascendant trine Uranus), Henry agreed to marry Arthur's widow, Catherine of Aragon, to retain her dowry. To marry her, Henry first needed a dispensation from the Pope, as his father had years before. With the death of his father, Henry VIII became king in April 1509 (Ascendant conjunct Mars) and seven weeks later was married, with the Pope's approval. The bride was five and a half years older than her husband and born December 16, 1485.

Henry desperately needed a male heir to secure the dynasty begun by his father. A son was born in early 1511 but lived only seven weeks. Other stillbirths followed until Mary was born in February 1516 (Ascendant trine Venus). Finally a son was born to one of his mistresses in 1519 (Earl of Richmond), but the child was illegitimate and had no legal claim to the throne.

Henry, a Cancer, had his eyes on forging a navy which would be the envy of the world. Henry also made inroads into France to reconquer that region won by Henry V a century before, but his attempts failed miserably. Henry turned his eyes to becoming the

Holy Roman Emperor, but was outvoted in the end.

When Martin Luther posted his ninety-five theses at Wittenberg in 1517, both Henry and his chief minister, Cardinal Wolsey, attacked Luther's theology. Henry even wrote a book condemning Lutheranism and the Pope considered conferring a title on Henry—"Defender of the Faith." When Catherine still failed to produce a male heir by 1527, Henry wanted a divorce on the grounds his marriage was invalid in that he had married his brother's widow. In other words, he wanted the Pope to annul his previous dispensation (Midheaven square Moon). Wolsey was told to cite passages from the Bible when conferring with the Pope. Catherine defended her honor, stating she was still a virgin when she married Henry and thus there was no incestuous union. Catherine was also afraid he would declare their daughter, Mary, illegitimate and thus remove her from the line of succession. Henry had his eye on Anne Boleyn, a lady-in-waiting to his wife and sister to one of Henry's former mistresses.

Anne was a rather attractive woman, sixteen years younger than Henry. She had a large mole on her neck and six fingers on her left hand; some called her a witch. Anne kept holding out for marriage, however long it took. Wolsey, failing to get the annulment from the Pope, was dismissed and stripped of all his powers. Henry took matters into his own hands (progressed Midheaven conjunct Sun), took over Wolsey's huge palace at Hampton Court, and worked out a deal with the English clergy which allowed him to become head of the Church of England.

On June 1, 1533, Henry had Anne crowned queen; she was six months pregnant and in September would bear a daughter whom they called Elizabeth (Ascendant square Sun). His former wife Catherine was place under house arrest, where she died in January 1536 (Ascendant sesquisquare Venus). By then, Henry had formally severed all ties with Rome and his divorce was made official by royal decree. Henry became the head of the Church of England in late November 1534.

Since Anne failed to produce a male heir, Henry had her falsely tried on grounds of adultery and she was beheaded in May 1536 (Midheaven opposite Uranus). Ten days later, Henry married Jane Seymour, a lady-in-waiting to his former wife Anne. Henry had both Mary and Elizabeth declared illegitimate a few months later. In October 1537, Jane produced the son Henry had so wanted. A fortnight alter, Jane died from complications of childbirth. Henry was devastated and by the end of 1539 signed a marriage contract by proxy with Anne of Cleves, whom he called the "Flanders mare." He disliked her on sight and a year later they divorced amicably, remaining friends for the remainder of his life. So much for mail order brides.

By July 1540, Henry had married again, this time to Catherine Howard, a cousin of Anne Boleyn. Catherine had many affairs prior to bedding with Henry, but the old king didn't seem to mind for he was in love again. But Catherine remained indiscreet and tales of her affairs could not be ignored, even though at first the king refused to acknowledge them. As adultery was a treasonable offense, Catherine was tried with a rigged court and found guilty. She was beheaded in February 1542 (Midheaven inconjunct Neptune sextile Mars). Henry didn't stay single for long. He married Catherine Parr the next year. She was twice widowed and engaged to Thomas Seymour at the time; in temperament she was more like a sister than a wife. She nursed Henry's gout and syphilitic leg and managed to reunite Henry with his two daughters. Henry died at 2:00 a.m. on January 28, 1547 (Midheaven sextile Venus square Pluto, Ascendant square Uranus), survived by three children and his wife, who later that year married her previously intended, Thomas Seymour.

At death, Henry was an enormous, bloated hulk of a man, a far cry from the smart and dashing figure of his youth. Cancer Suns often put on weight, but Henry's obesity certainly got out of hand. Mercury in Leo, as ruler of his Ascendant and Midheaven, made Henry a showman par excellence, a Renaissance prince of the first order. But Mercury's opposition to Saturn in the fifth house of love and affairs (Saturn also rules his fifth house) caused him much consternation when his wives could not bear the male heir he so desired. Jupiter, as co-ruler of the seventh house, in opposition to Neptune (modern ruler of the Descendant) caused his marital life to be disappointing. That two wives were beheaded and his third wife died in childbirth is shown by the square of Mars to the two planets ruling the Descendant, as Mars rules the eighth house of death.

Henry's conflicts with the Catholic church are shown by Venus in Gemini, ruler of the ninth house, semisquare the Sun, which put Henry at odds with religious authority figures. Venus is also inconjunct Pluto, indicating the path eventually taken: total elimination of the Papacy to gain Henry's desired aims. Henry destroyed many religious houses and confiscated several monasteries and nunneries, thus dividing England on religious matters. Despite this internal dissent, Henry did manage to weld together a nation as strong as any in Europe. His jovial, robust and self-indulgent nature endeared him to many despite the fact he could be totally irrational and bad tempered at times.

Edward VI

Edward VI, the only surviving son of Henry VIII and Jane Seymour, was born at Hampton Court on October 12, 1537 at 2:00 a.m. LAT (1:45 a.m. LMT) according to a biography by Chapman. His mother died two weeks after his birth (Neptune in the eighth house inconjunct the Ascendant and the Moon in the last degree of Capricorn square the Sun and sesquisquare Saturn). Edward was as different from his father as Henry VIII had been from his father. Edward was a small, frail-looking child, rather introverted and precocious (Mercury, ruler of the Ascendant, in Scorpio in the third house). Edward had a traumatic childhood, was reared by nurses, and had no family life until his father married Catherine Parr in 1543 (progressed Ascendant conjunct Venus). Edward was conversant in Greek, Latin and French and well versed in the religious reformation sweeping the continent. He was a serious boy, mature beyond his year but rather cold and distant to outsiders.

When his father died in January 1547, Edward was only nine (Midheaven sextile Uranus and Neptune trine Pluto; Ascendant semisquare Sun sesquisquare Moon) and the kingdom was placed under the protectorship of his uncle Edward Seymour, Duke of Somerset. His other uncle, Thomas Seymour, was accused of plotting to manipulate the succession and was beheaded for treason in 1549. Seymour had married Henry VIII's surviving wife, but she died in 1548 during childbirth. Before the end of 1549, the other uncle, Edward Seymour, was in the Tower of London for failing to stay the rebellions that erupted throughout England. Seymour lost

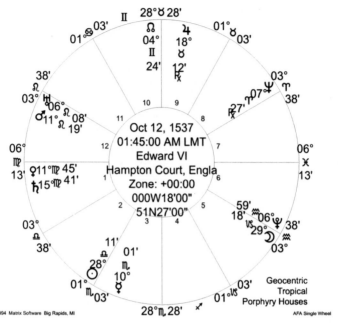

his head three years later.

Relations between Edward and his sister Mary worsened day by day with her stubborn insistence on keeping the old Catholic faith. *The Book of Common Prayer*, adopted in 1552, made England strongly Protestant, and laymen were severely punished for attending another form of worship. Edward's health was failing; he was never as robust as his father. Edward's bouts with smallpox and measles in the summer of 1552 took long to cure and the young king became weaker every day. Some said he inherited congenital syphilis from his late father. When his final illness, tuberculosis, made death imminent, religious factions battled for control of the kingdom. Few wanted Mary to succeed because she represented a return to the old days. Edward was determined that no Catholic would sit on his throne and named Lady Jane Grey as his successor. Jane was descended from Henry VIII's sister Mary and was Protestant. He went contrary to the will of his father, who had placed first Mary and then Elizabeth in line to the throne. Edward VI died July 6, 1553 (Midheaven sesquisquare Sun and Moon).

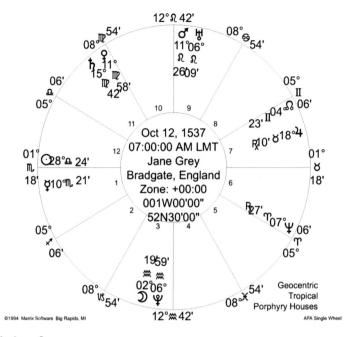

12° ♌ 42'

08° ♍ 54'
☿ 11°
♄ 15° ♍
♍ 42° 58'

06' ♎
05°

01° ♏
18' ☉ 28° ♎ 24'
☿ 10° ♏ 21'

05° ✕
06'

08° ♑
♑ 54'

♂ ♅
11° 06°
♌ ♌
26° 09'

10   9

11   8
    Oct 12, 1537
12 07:00:00 AM LMT 7
      Jane Grey
    Bradgate, England 6
      Zone: +00:00
2   001W00'00"
      52N30'00"   5
3   4

19° 59'
♒ ♒
02° 06°
☽ ♆

08° ♋ 54'

05°
♊
23' ♊ 04° ♋ 06'
♃ 0' ♉ 18° ♃

01°
♉
18'

♄ 27' ♈
07° ♆ 06'
♈
05°

08° ♓ 54'

12° ♒ 42'

Geocentric
Tropical
Porphyry Houses

©1994 Matrix Software Big Rapids, MI   AFA Single Wheel

Lady Jane Grey

Jane was born in Bradgate, Leicestershire on October 12, 1537, the same day as Edward VI, per data given in *Nine Days Queen* by Mary Luke. I've rectified the birth time to 7:15 a.m. LAT (7:00 a.m. LMT). Jane Grey was the daughter of the Duke of Suffolk, whose wife Frances was the daughter of Henry VIII's sister Mary. Thus, Henry VIII was her grand-uncle. Like her predecessor, Lady Jane was well versed in the classics and could read Greek, Latin and Hebrew. She married Guildford Dudley in the spring of 1553 and a few months later received news that she had been proclaimed queen upon the death of Edward VI (progressed Midheaven sextile Sun, Ascendant sextile Venus square Mars). The Duke of Northumberland, who forced the king to change his will, marched north to counterattack Princess Mary, but his support dwindled as Mary's grew. Jane was queen for only nine days until Mary took her rightful place in the line of succession. Jane was executed on February 12, 1554 with her husband. It was an unfortunate end for a woman who never wanted to be queen in the first place.

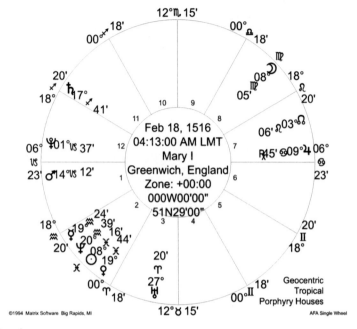

Feb 18, 1516
04:13:00 AM LMT
Mary I
Greenwich, England
Zone: +00:00
000W00'00"
51N29'00"

©1994 Matrix Software Big Rapids, MI

Geocentric
Tropical
Porphyry Houses

AFA Single Wheel

Mary I

Mary Tudor, the eldest surviving child of Henry VII and his first wife Catherine of Aragon, was born in Greenwich Palace on February 18, 1516 at 4:00 a.m. LAT (4:13 a.m. LMT), according to biographies by Jasper Ridley and Jean Plaidy. Mary's childhood was normal to age eleven when her parents decided to separate because her mother could not produce a male heir (progressed Midheaven sesquisquare Jupiter). Over the next few years, she witnessed her mother's humiliation by her father. By 1531, Mary was forbidden to even see her mother (Midheaven inconjunct Uranus). Two years later, after her father's remarriage to Anne Boleyn, Mary was declared a bastard (Midheaven semisquare Mars, Ascendant square Uranus). Three years later, her mother Catherine died in January 1536 (Ascendant semisquare Saturn). Later that year, Mary's stepmother was beheaded. One must wonder what resources Mary drew upon to deal with her father's subsequent marriages. Not until Catherine Parr came into the picture did Mary's domestic life improve. she was then reunited with her sister and brother

(Midheaven square Sun and Moon). In January 1547, her father died (Midheaven sesquisquare Jupiter, Ascendant conjunct Mercury and Neptune), leaving the throne to her younger brother, Edward VI.

After her brother's demise in the summer of 1533 (Midheaven sextile Mercury-Neptune square Venus), Mary rode to London, gathering her support as successor to her father's throne and had the usurper, Lady Jane Grey, arrested for treason, sent to the Tower and later executed. Being an ardent and devout Catholic, Mary sought to eradicate any vestiges of the "new religion" by rounding up leading churchmen and putting them in the Tower. Thus began a series of religious persecutions which earned her the nickname "Bloody Mary." Even her sister Elizabeth was under suspicion for her admiration of Archbishop Cranmer. After Elizabeth spent two months in confinement, Mary released her from the Tower.

Mary's choice of Philip II, King of Spain, as her marriage partner made her reign even more unpopular. Her husband was eleven years her junior and a widower. Like Mary, he was a staunch Catholic and quite familiar with tactics used by the Inquisition to deal with heretics. As King of England, many felt he would treat his wife's country as just another colony. Their union took place in Winchester Cathedral in July 1554 (Ascendant opposite Moon, ruler of Descendant), beginning a rivalry between England and Spain which would culminate during the attack of the Spanish Armada three decades later. Mary then petitioned the Pope for reconciliation with Rome, thus allowing for more persecution of Protestants. Mary had a false pregnancy resulting in only a phantom delivery. Philip rapidly grew tired of Mary and paid more attention to her sister Elizabeth. Philip was the most powerful man in Europe, governing an empire that ruled much of the Americas along with the Netherlands and the Kingdom of Naples. Philip left Mary at the end of the summer of 1555 and all her appeals for his return fell on deaf ears. With Jupiter in her seventh house trine the Sun, one might have presumed her married life more pleasant than it actually was. But marital difficulties are reflected in the ruler of the Descendant (the Moon) opposing the Sun. Mary went on with her persecutions, even burning Archbishop Cranmer at the stake. Disputes with the Pope continued due to the new Pope's hatred of the English legate to the Holy See, who was also in line to be Pope. Meanwhile, Philip returned briefly to manipulate Mary into going to war with Spain against France, Spain's arch enemy. Philip also tried to persuade Elizabeth to marry the Duke of Savoy so the crown wouldn't' fall into French hands via the Stuart line.

In January 1558, the French captured Calais, the last English possession in France. Four centuries before, when Henry II came to the throne, his estates and those of his rich wife Eleanor made them the largest landowners in Europe. The fall of Calais was a sad note in English history.

Mary died at 6:00 a.m. on November 17, 1558 (Ascendant square Saturn, ruler of her Ascendant) and being childless, she left the throne to her sister she so detested. Mary's traumatic childhood left her wary and insecure, albeit precocious. Always strong willed and stubborn, with Pluto rising, she was a pious woman (Sun trine Jupiter) but plain and dull in appearance. She had a grave demeanor with piercing eyes and auburn hair (like her father) atop a slight and delicate frame. Unlike her sister Elizabeth, she was no raving beauty. Mary's ruthlessness may be attributed to Scorpio ruling her Midheaven and its ruler, Pluto, sitting so close to her Ascendant. Had Mary lived in another age, she might have been better remembered. But that Sun-Moon opposition square Saturn (ruler of her Ascendant) made her life one of trouble, hate and discord. She was a zealot who caused 280 to be burned at the stake to satisfy her religious fanaticism.

Elizabeth I

Elizabeth Tudor was born on a Sunday afternoon at Greenwich Palace on September 7, 1533. Most biographies state she was born between 3:00 and 4:00 p.m., giving her Capricorn rising like her sister. *Notable Nativities* by Alan Leo gives the time as 2:30 p.m. LAT (2:24 p.m. LMT) and a late Sagittarius rising, which I think fits the course of her life much better than the later birth times.

When Elizabeth was three, her mother, Anne Boleyn, was beheaded for treason (progressed Midheaven opposite Moon). Elizabeth grew up fearing the father who had declared her a bastard. Her father's sixth marriage, to Catherine Parr, made Elizabeth's domestic life more tranquil after 1543, except for her stepmother's

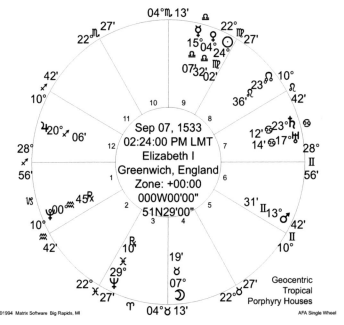

Chart details:
04°♏︎13' ♎︎
22°♏︎27'
☿ 15°♎︎04' ♀ ☉ 22°♍︎27'
24°♎︎
07°♎︎32'02'♍︎
42'
10° ♐︎
23°♌︎10'
♌︎42'
36'♋︎
♃20°♐︎06'
28° ♐︎
56'
12° Sep 07, 1533
02:24:00 PM LMT
Elizabeth I
Greenwich, England
Zone: +00:00
000W00'00"
51N29'00"
12°♋︎23°♄ ♋︎
14'♋︎17°♉︎♅
28° ♊︎
56'
♑︎ ♇00°♒︎45°℞
10° ♒︎
42'
31' ♊︎13°♂
42' ♊︎
10°
℞ 10°♉︎
♓︎29°♃
22°♓︎27'♃
♈︎ 04°♉︎13' ☽
19' ♉︎07°
22°♉︎27'

Geocentric
Tropical
Porphyry Houses
AFA Single Wheel

former fiancé, Thomas Seymour, who kept making passes at her (Ascendant trine Moon). In January 1547, her father died, leaving the throne to her younger brother Edward VI (Midheaven trine Uranus). Six year later, her brother died, her elder sister Mary became queen and Elizabeth was thrown in prison (Midheaven trine Saturn sextile Sun). After the long awaited death of her "bloody" sister in 1558, Young Bess came to the throne she was to rule for the next forty-five years (Midheaven trine Neptune).

Elizabeth began her reign as the most popular monarch in recent memory. Her coronation on the date chosen by astrologer John Dee was one of the most glorious and festive occasions England had seen in years. Being single and with no strong contender for her affections, Elizabeth was the most eligible catch in Europe. The matchmakers got busy and a host of suitors trekked in for inspection. This strong willed woman was a feminist of sorts with an independent mind and no desire to be rushed into marriage. She declared, one year after becoming queen, that she was content to remain a virgin. The Moon in Taurus was quite stubborn and its square to Pluto doubled the armor. The Sun in the ninth house square Jupiter also sextiled Saturn, giving Elizabeth resiliency and the inability to bend to pressure. She felt England was her mate and she could not effectively rule her country were she to divide her time with a husband. Note Uranus in the seventh house square Mercury, ruler of the Descendant for further confirmation.

Elizabeth was a vain and haughty woman, always dressed in the latest fashions, adorned by strands of jewelry and tons of makeup. Like many fire sign women, Elizabeth started to lose her hair at an early age but the plentitude of wigs at her disposal covered up any embarrassment her baldness might cause. In 1562 she overcame a bout with smallpox that would have destroyed a weaker individual. Like her father, Elizabeth had tons of vigor and seldom tired of the many demands her job required. She ruled with a high degree of intelligence (speaking seven languages) and a great deal of good judgment, and remained open to any new cultural attraction. Her flirtatious ways made her fascinating despite a bad temper that often surfaced.

By her first Saturn return in 1563, Elizabeth was forced to acknowledge that she had taken no vows of celibacy after members of Parliament became increasingly worried about her succession. Her closest living relative was Mary, Queen of Scots, who sought haven in England in 1568 and was a Catholic. Mary's entrance into England after her abdication in Scotland created a diplomatic imbroglio (Midheaven sesquisquare Saturn, Ascendant trine Mars). The coup in Scotland had put Mary's son James VI on the throne; fortunately, he was a Protestant and would, at Elizabeth's death, rule England as well.

With Elizabeth's Ascendant conjunct the Uranus of the English horoscope, it's no wonder exploration and foreign adventure became a byword for the Elizabethan Age. Sir Frances Drake was sent around the world in 1577 (Midheaven conjunct Jupiter) and seven years later, Sir Walter Raleigh tried unsuccessfully to build a colony at Roanoke in the Americas (Midheaven square Sun). Meanwhile, English ships were pirating Spanish treasure, creating a further rift between England and Spain. England allied with France against Spain in 1571 as Catholic uprisings at home placed Elizabeth's position in jeopardy. Elizabeth came close to marrying Lord Dudley, the Earl of Leicester, but instead sent him to the Tower after he married another in secret.

By 1586, Philip of Spain was planning war against England to counteract repeated pirating of Spanish ships. Due to his marriage with Mary Tudor, he still believed he was rightfully King of England. An armada of 600 ships was to include forty-five galleons, the date of the invasion yet to be determined. After Mary, Queen of Scots, was found guilty of treason for partaking in the abortive Babington plot to assassinate the queen, she was executed at Fotheringay Castle in February 1587. This was the last straw for Philip, who now had more than enough reason to invade England. But Elizabeth didn't jump for joy at the news that her rival was gone. Even after signing a death warrant, she felt there must be another way to dealing with Mary. Later that summer Drake burned tons of provisions meant for the Spanish Armada and made Philip even more furious.

The great Spanish Armada sailed from Lisbon on May 30, 1588 with 130 ships carrying 17,000 soldiers. Delayed by storms, the fleet was first sighted off the southwest coast of England on July 19. Over the next ten days, the English engaged the Spanish four times as they tried to reach Calais to pick up more troops. The English attacked with fire and other explosives and soon the fleet was scattered due to high winds. Two days later, the fleet was in retreat, around the north end of Scotland on its way home. The Spanish lost eleven ships and more than 2,000 men. The English lost 50 men and no ships. This was the greatest glory of Elizabeth's reign. Despite Elizabeth's progressed Midheaven squaring Neptune at the time, it was the victory that showed Europe that England was no longer a second-rate power.

The last 15 years of Elizabeth's reign were relatively peaceful with the threat of Spanish invasion crushed. This was the flowering age of men like Shakespeare, Bacon, Marlowe, Spenser, Gibbons and Byrd. It was also possibly the last time Elizabeth allowed herself to fall in love, this time with Robert Devereaux, the Earl of Essex, a man half her age. Abandoning his mission in Ireland in 1599, he was placed under house arrest for plotting to take over the position of chief minister. His beheading in February 1601 left Elizabeth disconsolate. Elizabeth died at 3:00 a.m. on March 24, 1603 at age 69, having ruled England for 45 years (progressed Ascendant square Pluto, Midheaven inconjunct Mars).

Physically, Elizabeth was striking rather than beautiful. Despite her overwhelming vanity, she couldn't hide her long fingers and hooked nose. She often swallowed arsenic to make her skin look pale. Her auburn hair faded to white and in later years she went totally bald. Always regal and confident (Sun square Ascendant), her high and mighty ways endeared her to those privileged enough to gain entrance to her splendid and magnificent court. She lacked her sister's fanaticism, possibly due to the Mercury in Libra which likes to weigh all sides of an issue before making judgment. Elizabeth's many lovers might be shown by Venus ruling the fifth house in Libra, but her inability to get serious over any of her suitors is due to Venus inconjunct the Moon (co-ruler of her house of marriage). Elizabeth was always interested in expanding English horizons. That is typical of an individual with Sagittarius rising; its ruler, Jupiter, was rising above the Ascendant. Her tireless work for her country is shown by Mars in the sixth house, trine the ruler of that house. Her refusal to let any one man run her life (unlike her sister) is illustrated by Saturn and Uranus in her seventh house. Elizabeth was a remarkable woman to be certain, the likes of which England has not seen since. During her reign, England became a powerful force and a country secure from foreign invasion. Elizabeth marked the end of the Tudor dynasty; the throne now passed to the Stuarts, who ruled both England and Scotland.

The Stuarts

Mary, Queen of Scots

Mary, Queen of Scots, was born December 7, 1542 in Linlithgow, Scotland at 1:30 p.m. LAT, according to *Nativitas* by Martin Harvey. I've rectified the time to 1:26 p.m. LAT (1:23 p.m. LMT). Her father, James V, died when she was a week old, making her Queen of Scotland. Her grandmother, Margaret Tudor, was daughter to Henry VII and sister to Henry VIII, making Elizabeth I of England her cousin. The early demise of her father is shown by the Midheaven at birth sesquisquare Uranus and the Ascendant opposing Saturn, ruler of the Midheaven.

Mary fled to France in 1548 where she remained for the next dozen years. While there, she married Francis II, the Dauphin of France, in 1558 (progressed Midheaven sextile Venus). When Henry II was killed in a jousting battle (as predicted by Nostradamus) the following July, her husband became king (progressed Ascendant trine Pluto). But her reign as Queen of France was short lived as her husband died in December 1560 (Ascendant inconjunct Saturn); six months later, her mother, Mary of Guise, passed away.

When she returned to Scotland the next year, her Catholic beliefs encountered resistance from the Scottish reformation, then in full force. In July 1565, Mary wed her half-cousin, Lord Darnley,

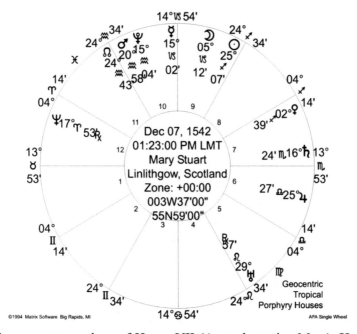

14°♑54'

24°♒34'   ♂♅15°   ☿15°   ☽05°   ☉24°♐34'
24° ♌20° ♒   ♑   ♑   25°
♓   ♒   43'58'04'   02'   12'   07'
14'   04°
♈   10   9   ♐14'
04°
♅17°♈53℞   11   39'♐02°♀
13°   12   Dec 07, 1542   8   04°
♉   01:23:00 PM LMT   7   24°♏16°♄13°
53'   Mary Stuart   ♏
1   Linlithgow, Scotland   6   53'
Zone: +00:00   27'♎25°♃
2   003W37'00"   5
55N59'00"   14'
04°   3   4   ♎
♊   04°
14'   ℞
♏7'
♌29°
♅
24°   34'   Geocentric
♊34'   24°♌   Tropical
14°♋54'   Porphyry Houses

©1994 Matrix Software Big Rapids, MI

AFA Single Wheel

also a great-grandson of Henry VII (Ascendant trine Mars). Her husband, as King of Scotland, so enraged and alienated the court because of his overt vanity, pomposity and general rudeness, that in February 1567 he was killed in a massive bomb explosion. The chief suspect, the Earl of Bothwell, became Mary's third husband three months later (Midheaven semisquare Sun) he abducted her to his castle, where some say he raped her. Considering that Bothwell was probably Mary's lover during the last days of her marriage to Darnley, this rumor seems farfetched. The nobles rose up in arms in July 1567 and Mary abdicated the throne, leaving her son of thirteen months as King of Scotland. One year later, Mary sought sanctuary in England (Ascendant opposite Sun trine Jupiter) where her presence was a constant source of worry and concern to her cousin Elizabeth I. After eighteen and a half years of imprisonment, Mary's death warrant was reluctantly signed by Elizabeth after Mary was implicated in the Babington Plot to overthrow the English queen. Mary was executed at Fotheringay Castle on February 8, 1587 (progressed Midheaven opposite Uranus), meeting her end with dignity and forgiving her executioner.

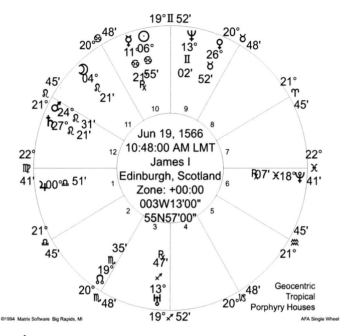

Chart data:
- 19° ♊ 52'
- 20° ♋ 48'
- ☿ ⊙ 11° 06° ♋ ♋
- 24° 21' ♃° ♌
- 2 55' ♋ R♃
- 13° ♆ ♊ 26° 02' ♀ 52' ♉
- 20° ♉ 48'
- 45' ♌ 21° ♂ 24° ♌ ☊27° ♌ 31' 21'
- 21° ♈ 45'
- 22° ♍ 41' ♄00° ♎ 51'
- Jun 19, 1566 10:48:00 AM LMT James I Edinburgh, Scotland Zone: +00:00 003W13'00" 55N57'00"
- 22° ♓ 41'
- ♅07' ♓18' ♇
- 21° ♎ 45'
- 45' ♒ 21°
- 35' 19° ♏ ☋ 20° ♏ 48'
- R 47' 13° ♑ ♅
- 48' 20° ♑
- 19° ♐ 52'
- Geocentric Tropical Porphyry Houses

©1994 Matrix Software Big Rapids, MI

AFA Single Wheel

James I

James was born in Edinburgh Castle, Scotland, on June 19, 1566 between 10:00 and 11:00 a.m. according to biographies by Charles Williams and Antonia Fraser. I've rectified his birth time to 10:45 a.m. LAT (10:48 a.m. LMT). His mother was the tragic Mary, Queen of Scots; his father, Lord Darnley, was murdered when James was less than eight months old (progressed Midheaven semisquare Moon).

Due to Mary's son James' youth and inexperience, power rested in the hands of the Duke of Lenox, much to the dislike of the Scottish nobility. The young king was kidnaped in July 1582, a year after the Earl of Morton was executed for the murder of James' father, Lord Darnley (progressed Ascendant sextile Moon). It's not known how James felt about his mother's execution in 1587 (Midheaven semisquare Mars, Ascendant square Sun) because they hadn't seen each other since he was in infant.

In August 1589, James wed Anne of Denmark (born December 12, 1574) by proxy (Midheaven semisquare Venus). It was an odd

123

match for Anne was an incorrigible flirt and her husband was notoriously bisexual. She not only had to put up with his male favorites, but had to approve of them before James would sleep with them. Anne was often irritable and in poor health, but James did his royal duty and produced two heirs (Princes Henry and Charles) and a daughter who wed the Elector of the Palatinate from which the Hanover dynasty was descended.

James VI of Scotland became King James I of England on the death of Queen Elizabeth in March 1603 (Ascendant inconjunct Pluto). The transition was smoother than anticipated and the English welcomed their new monarch with open arms. Compared to the glory of the Elizabethan Age, James' coronation was a no-frills affair due to his Virgo rising love of simplicity and privacy. But opposition to his rule was fomenting and erupted in the Gunpowder Plot of November 1605 in which Guy Fawkes planned to blow up Parliament while the king was opening that August body (Midheaven semisquare Neptune sesquisquare Uranus). The conspiracy was uncovered in time and Fawkes was executed three months later. During his reign, the New World was settled at Jamestown in 1607 and by the Puritans in 1620. Meanwhile, James' wife Anne died in March 1619 of dropsy (progressed Ascendant inconjunct Venus sesquisquare Neptune); he had ceased living with her many years earlier. James died on March 27, 1625 (progressed Midheaven semisquare Jupiter).

Like the Stuart kings before him, James believed in his "divine right to rule" rather than just to reign. He detested interference from Parliament, which he often considered useless. Mars and Saturn in his twelfth point to the many enemies made during his reign and the Mars and Saturn squares to Venus indicate the continued religious factionalism he had to endure. James was a shrewd monarch due to that foxy Virgo Ascendant. It also gave him many health problems. Note Pluto in his sixth house square both Uranus (ruler of the sixth house) and Neptune, and Neptune sesquisquare the Moon as well. James had weak and spindly legs and in later years was almost an invalid. His temperament was shy and timorous and he was prone to severe bouts of insomnia (Saturn in the twelfth house?). He probably would have been happier as a scholar or theologian, for under his rule the famed Bible that bears his name was first published. Always bookish and introverted, James wrote treatises on tobacco and on religious matters and believed in witches and demons (Mercury inconjunct Uranus?). James was a crude man whose oversized tongue caused him to drool and slobber while eating.

The extremes of his personality might be explained by Pluto opposing the Ascendant. While he could ramble about the most arcane of topics, he would often present ideas in language that would make a sailor blush. James was alternatively lazy, vain and extravagant due to the Moon in Leo, yet his reign was largely one of peace because of his political savvy. His licentiousness was a source of embarrassment to most and in his final days he was called the ``wisest fool in Christendom'' by the King of France. He left a legacy of distrust between the Crown and Parliament which escalated into civil war during the reign of his son Charles I.

Charles I

Charles was born at Dunfermline, Scotland on November 19, 1600 O.S. (November 29, 1600 N.S.) at 10;05 p.m. LAT (9:54 p.m. LMT), with my rectification. Other sources gave the time as 10:00 p.m. (including Charles Harvey and Alan Leo), while Gadbury uses a time two minutes earlier. Charles was a frail and sickly child and grew up under the shadow of his brother Henry, Prince of Wales. When his brother died in 1612 (progressed Midheaven inconjunct Venus), Charles was unprepared to assume the kingly role. Charles was very shy, had a mild speech defect (stammering) and was rather reserved and grave (Pluto trine the Ascendant with a rising Neptune). His mother Anne died when he was eighteen (Midheaven square Neptune, Ascendant square Sun) and six years later is father passed away (Midheaven trine Moon inconjunct Saturn).

One of his first acts as king was to marry Henrietta Maria, daughter of the King of France. Born November 15, 1609, she was a hot tempered and strong willed woman who refused to be crowned with her husband because of her strong Catholic beliefs. Her large eyes and flashing smile contrasted sharply with her husband's shy and backward nature. Nine years younger than Charles, she was very short, reaching only his shoulder—and Charles was only 5'4"! Henrietta Maria continually meddled in affairs of state,

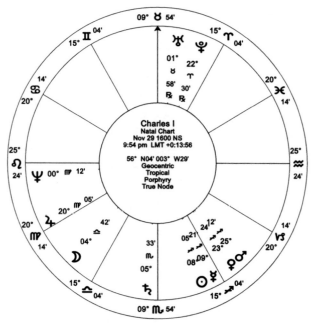

had a strong hold on her husband, and continually scolded their six children. She was also highly jealous of her husband's favorite, the Duke of Buckingham. Charles' Descendant ruler Uranus opposes Saturn, which accounts for many of his wife's strong traits.

Buckingham was implicated in a plot to pawn a collection of royal jewelry (as written about by Dumas in *The Three Musketeers*) and Charles disbanded Parliament to save his friend's hide. But Buckingham's mission to aid the Hugenots, combined with fears of growing Catholicism at court because of Charles' wife, caused Buckingham to be assassinated in 1628 following a rumored plot to kill the queen. One year later, in March 1629, Charles disbanded Parliament after it challenged his authority to rule (progressed Midheaven opposite Mercury, ruler of the eleventh house of Parliament; progressed Ascendant sesquisquare Uranus, ruler of the seventh house of open enemies). Despite the differences between Charles and his wife, after Buckingham's death the royal couple became much closer.

For the next 11 years, Charles ruled England without the aid of Parliament. When it did reconvene in 1640, Charles again dissolved it (progressed Midheaven square Jupiter). Meanwhile, Charles had to deal with Scottish dissenters and his wife's rumored secret diplomacy with Catholic monarchs on the Continent made her a hostage in England.

The year 1642 began with Charles' fury with Parliament for attempting to impeach the queen and his arrest of five members of that body. But Londoners rose up and Charles was forced to flee the city. The queen fled to the Low Countries to seek financial and military aid for her husband's cause. By summer, the first seeds of civil war had erupted (progressed Midheaven opposite Venus sextile Pluto, Ascendant square Mars). The next four years were tumultuous and Charles was finally captured by the Scots and handed over to Parliament in January 1647. But Parliament had a new threat to its survival—the army, which began to march on London. In December 1648, the army occupied London and soldiers seized the king, taking him to the Isle of Wight for protection.

Parliament condemned Charles I for treason on January 27, 1649; three days later he was beheaded (Midheaven sextile Neptune). Six weeks later, the Monarchy was abolished and a motion was passed to make England a commonwealth under the rule of the House of Commons. England was ruled by the forty-one member Council of State until Oliver Cromwell formally took the reins of power.

Despite Charles' efforts to be a good and upright ruler, his arrogant and stubborn manner did little to endear him to his subjects. Leo rising (and possibly his Sun combust Mercury) made him blind to his faults. Saturn in the third house gave him little humor and no doubt limited his mental perspectives. Charles was a man of strong prejudices whose poor judgment (Jupiter semisquare Saturn inconjunct Pluto) nearly tore England asunder. But Charles did have a sensitive and aesthetic side for he amassed a vast collection of art. Always autocratic, inflexible and completely lacking in imagination, he is remembered as a haughty king who had little comprehension of the democratic way of life.

Oliver Cromwell

Cromwell was born in Huntingdon, England on April 25, 1599 O.S. (May 5, 1599 N.S.) at 3:00 a.m. LAT (2:56 a.m. LMT), ac-

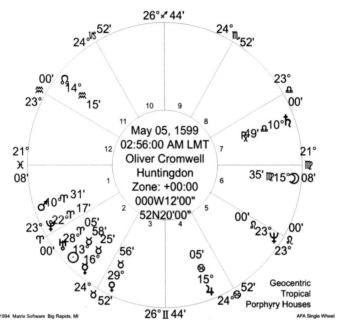

26°♐44'

24°♑52'

24°♏52'

00' ♒ ♌4°♒
23° 15'

26°♐44' (MC)

23° ♎ 00'

♇49' ♎10°♄

10 9

11 8

May 05, 1599
02:56:00 AM LMT
Oliver Cromwell
Huntingdon
Zone: +00:00
000W12'00"
52N20'00"

21° ♓ 12 7 21° ♍
08' 1 6 35' ♍15'☽08'

♂10°♈31'
♀22°♈17'
23° ♇ ♈ ♈05'
♈ ♃28°♈58'
00' ♅13°♉25'
☉16°♉ 56'
♉ 29°

24° ♉ 05°
♀52' ☊15°
♃52'
24°☊52'

00' ☊23°♆ 00'
♆ ♌
23°

Geocentric
Tropical
Porphyry Houses

©1994 Matrix Software Big Rapids, MI

26°♊44'

AFA Single Wheel

cording to his mother. Married at age 20 (Midheaven opposite Jupiter trine Moon), he achieved prominence during the civil war that erupted in 1642 (Ascendant sextile Mars trine Saturn). Cromwell was a man of superior military ability who picked his troops with respect, not only for their ability on the battle field but also for their religion. Note that Mars rises and is opposed by Saturn for the confirmation of this military acumen.

During his brief stint as ruler of England, which began in 1649 (Midheaven inconjunct Moon and Jupiter, Ascendant sextile Pluto), he was a dictator who made his homeland a virtual police state. Pluto rising points to his ability to command love and reverence as well as hate and fear. Nobody was ambivalent about Cromwell.

Note that Jupiter sextiles the Sun and Moon, one of the luckiest combos possible in a chart. When Cromwell was offered the title of king, he refused, being in essence more democratic than the man he deposed. Cromwell's efforts to work with Parliament became a strain over the year, especially after he was installed as Lord Protector in December 1653.

128

During the summer of 1658, Cromwell's daughter died and he went into severe depression from which he never recovered. Cromwell passed away on September 3, 1658 (Midheaven opposite Neptune, Ascendant sextile Uranus), leaving the reins of power in the hands of his son Richard, who was chosen over Cromwell's elder brother in hopes England could avoid another dictator. But Richard never received the support of the army and thus resigned his post as Lord Protector in May 1659. Richard Cromwell died an old man in 1712 at age 86. England was a commonwealth for another year until the Stuart Restoration placed Charles II on the throne in May 1660.

Charles II

Charles II was born in London on May 29, 1630 O.S. (June 8, 1630 N.S.) at high noon LAT (11:58 a.m. LMT), according to *Royal Charles* by Antonia Fraser. In looks, Charles was an ugly baby, dark and swarthy like his mother. Temperamentally, he was lazy and profligate, the complete opposite of his father. When the civil war began in 1642 (progressed Midheaven trine Saturn), his life was spent on the run for six and a half years until his father was beheaded in January 1649 (Midheaven semisquare Moon, Ascendant semisquare Mars sesquisquare Pluto). Despite England's becoming a commonwealth, Charles was offered the crown of Scotland if he would convert to Presbyterianism, which he did in January 1651. Shortly thereafter, he fled to France after Cromwell's troops placed a price on his head (Midheaven sextile Venus). Charles lived in France for the next nine years until Parliament decided to restore the monarchy. Charles entered London on his thirtieth birthday (Ascendant inconjunct Jupiter). He took immediate steps to heal the wounds of the previous decade; before long, life was jubilant and harmony prevailed.

In May 1662, Charles married Catherine of Braganza, daughter of the King of Portugal. Born November 25, 1638, she came with a huge dowry of 350,000 pounds, which included Tangier and Bombay. Despite being Catholic, she agreed to rear her children as Protestants, a moot point as the couple would have no children. Preferring to remain naive about her husband's numerous affairs, Catherine was always kind to his many bastard children. The fact

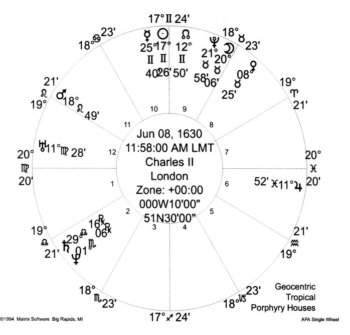

17°♊24'

18°♋23'

☿ ☉ ☊
25°17° 12°
♊ ♊ ♊
40°26'50'

18°♉23'

♆ ☽
21° 20°
♉ ♉
58'06'

19°♈21'

25'

♂18°♌49'

21'
♌
19°

♅11°♍28'

20°
♍
20'

10   9

11   8

Jun 08, 1630
11:58:00 AM LMT
Charles II
London
Zone: +00:00
000W10'00"
51N30'00"

12   7

1   6

2   5

3   4

20°
♍
X

52'♓11°♃ 20°
20'

19°
♎
21'

♇16°♏
29°06°
♄♍01°♏

21'
♒
19°

18°♏23'

18°♑23'

17°♐24'

Geocentric
Tropical
Porphyry Houses

©1994 Matrix Software Big Rapids, MI

AFA Single Wheel

that Charles had no legitimate children might be shown by the
Sun-Jupiter square opposing Saturn, the planet of status. Catherine
was a tiny woman, considerably shorter than her husband, who
stood 6'2" tall. She was dark like Charles' mother but rather plump
in her later years. Always patient, self-controlled and very obliging, Catherine was a pious and reserved woman whose personality
contrasted sharply with that of her licentious mate.

During the first decade of Charles II's reign, England endured
the Plague of 1665, which brought foreign trade to a standstill. The
next year London went up in flames (Midheaven sextile Pluto, Ascendant sextile Sun), but soon a new and more beautiful London
emerged from the ashes with Christopher Wren as chief architect.
Three years after the Great Fire of 1666, Charles' mother died
(Midheaven semisquare Uranus sesquisquare Jupiter, Ascendant
inconjunct Moon).

Despite Charles' attempts to mollify and pacify religious ex-
tremists, a plot was uncovered in 1678 whereby Irish ruffians were
to either shoot or poison the king. Catholic homes were searched
for arms and the chief suspect was none other than his brother

James, the Duke of York, When Charles fell seriously ill the following year, the House of Commons was determined that no Catholic would ever again wear the crown. James had secretly converted to Catholicism, so to placate Parliament, he was exiled to Scotland for a year. Some supported the king's eldest bastard son, the Duke of Monmouth, who was eventually exiled to the Low Countries after being convicted in a plot to overthrow his father. On his deathbed, Charles II did convert to Catholicism. He asked James to look after his favorite mistress, Nell Gwyn, shortly before he died on February 6, 1685 (Midheaven semisquare Mercury, Ascendant conjunct Saturn). His son, the Duke of Monmouth, was executed for treason five months later.

Charles was a sophisticated and intelligent man (Sun in Gemini), always kind, considerate and charming (Moon in Taurus). He had a lighthearted sense of humor (Mercury in Gemini) and considerable tolerance, but in reality was always a dabbler and dilettante due to those four mutable angles. The T-square involving the Sun, Jupiter and Uranus made him continually restless, always seeking adventure, excitement and variety. Charles' reputation as a ladies' man was beyond parallel: He was reputed to have had 39 mistresses and 20 illegitimate children. That Moon-Pluto conjunction with Venus in Taurus gave him a large sexual appetite, doubly so with Mars square the Moon and Pluto.

His reign was one of lassitude, indulgence and debauchery, a time of intense physical pleasure to counteract the Puritan ways of the previous decades. Charles was never a passive lover, unlike other monarchs who believed women should serve them. According to folklore, Charles was very well-endowed sexually. It's said that our basic unit of measure, the foot, was due to the fact that Charles had a 12-inch appendage. So much for the metric system. One should also note that Mercury, ruler of the Ascendant and Midheaven, trines Saturn, ruler of the fifth house of love and romance. Charles loved England (especially the ladies) and England returned the favor. He was a popular monarch despite his tendency at times to be sardonic, calculating and vindictive to those who thwarted his ambitions.

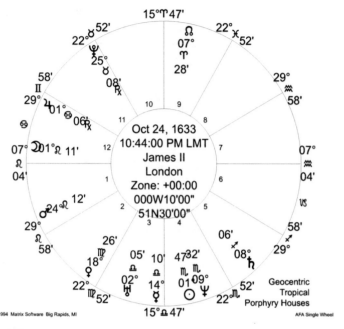

15°♈47'

22°♂52'   ☊ 07° ♈ 28'   22°♓52'

♆ 25°♂   08' ♀℞   29° ♒ 58'

58' Ⅱ 29°♃   01° 06'℞⊗   10   9

⊗   11   8   07° ♒ 04'

07°♋ ☽01°♌11'   12   Oct 24, 1633
10:44:00 PM LMT
James II
London
Zone: +00:00
000W10'00"
51N30'00"   7

♌ 04'   1   6   ♍

24° ♌12' ♂   2   5   58' ♐

29° ♌58'   3   4   06'   29° ♐

26' ♍ 18° ♀   05' 10' 47°32'   08' ♄   52'

22° ♍52'   02' ♎ ♅ 14° ☊   01°09' ♏ ♏ ☉ ♆   22°♏   Geocentric
Tropical
Porphyry Houses

©1994 Matrix Software Big Rapids, MI   15°♎47'   AFA Single Wheel

James II

James II was born in London on October 14, 1633 O.S. (October 24, 1633 N.S.) at 11:00 p.m. LAT (10:44 p.m. LMT), according to Martin Harvey. During the last days of his father's reign, James escaped to Holland dressed as a woman (Midheaven square Moon sextile Jupiter). In January 1649, his father was beheaded for treason (Midheaven opposite Sun). Shortly after his brother, Charles II, restored the monarchy, James secretly wed Anne Hyde in October 1660 (Midheaven inconjunct Mercury, Ascendant square Pluto). Eight years later he converted to Catholicism (Ascendant sextile Jupiter), an act which, because he was the sole heir, caused considerable worry in Parliament. His mother died the next year (Ascendant sextile Sun). Anne Hyde passed away at age 34 in late March 1671 (Midheaven square Mars), leaving James with two young girls. Two years later, in 1673, James married Mary of Modena (born October 5, 1658) shortly after he resigned his post as lord high admiral (Midheaven conjunct Pluto). The second marriage caused even greater political repercussions as his new wife was a staunch Catholic: The threat of another Catholic on the throne drove Parliament into a frenzy. The Test Act, passed in late 1673, limited the power of any future Catholic monarch and barred any Papist from sitting in Parliament. It was even suggested that Charles II divorce his wife and remarry to ensure a Protestant succession. True to his stubborn, arrogant self, James refused to take the Test Act oath.

After the abortive Popish Plot of 1678, James was linked to the conspiracy and exiled to Scotland for a year. With the death of his brother, James became king in February 1685 (Midheaven opposite Saturn), the first Catholic to sit on the throne since Mary Tudor. James believed in the "divine right of kings," just as his forebears had. The question of a Catholic succession wasn't of prime importance and the king and his second wife had no children. In the wings stood his daughter Mary and her Dutch husband, William of Orange, who became even more attractive after the penal laws against Catholics were suspended in 1687. After James II received the Pope, a volcano started to rumble, erupting in full force when his wife Mary gave birth to a son in June 1688 (Ascendant semisquare Sun and Moon). Since his wife had lost four children in infancy and had undergone several miscarriages, it was rumored the baby was not the queen's at all, but smuggled into her bedchamber in a warming pan. Three weeks later, a conspiracy arose to oust James and the nobles asked William of Orange to lead an invasion to depose the king.

William of Orange landed in England in November 1688 and within six weeks James fled to France. He had tried to leave two weeks earlier, dressed in disguise, but dropped the Great Seal into the Thames. William ordered James out of England permanently. James tried to regain his throne in the summer of 1690 at the Battle of Boyne, but was hopelessly defeated. James retired to France, where he died at St. Germain on September 6, 1707 (Midheaven sextile Mars, Ascendant trine Pluto).

With the exception of Kings John, Richard II and Edward II, no English monarch was so detested and reviled as James II. He was a tactless and abrasive man (Sun in Scorpio) with an arrogant streak a mile wide (Ascendant in Leo). His rigidity and dourness did little to endear him to the English and his impatience and irritability were legendary. James was a pious man who took his faith seriously, but his choice of religion sealed his fate (Neptune, ruler of the ninth house, squared his Ascendant). James was a loving and devoted husband despite the fact that he was just as oversexed as his brother and had many mistresses. In the end, he simply couldn't or wouldn't bend with the times (fixed position of the Sun, Moon and Ascendant).

Mary II

Mary Stuart was born in London on April 30, 1662 O.S. (May 10, 1662 N.S.) at 1:00 a.m. LAT (12:56 a.m. LMT), according to *William's Mary* by Elizabeth Hamilton. Mary was barely nine years old when her mother, Anne Hyde, passed away (progressed Ascendant square Sun) and within two years she had Mary of Modena as stepmother. Mary wed her cousin, William of Orange, in November 1677 (Midheaven inconjunct Sun, ruler of Descendant). During the ceremony she continually cried as her husband was not the "man of her dreams"; first, they would have to live in Holland, and second, her husband was half a foot shorter. Despite

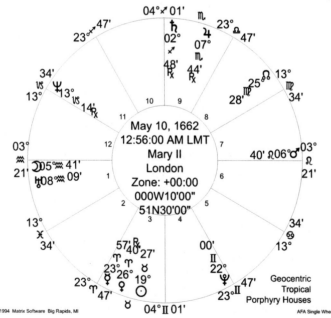

©1994 Matrix Software Big Rapids, MI

Geocentric
Tropical
Porphyry Houses

AFA Single Wheel

being an arranged union, in time Mary grew to worship and adore her husband (Leo on the seventh house cusp). Note also that Mars in the seventh house sextiles Saturn but opposes her rising Moon and Uranus for confirmation of her initial revulsion.

After her father's second wife gave birth to a son in the spring of 1688, the nobles asked Mary's husband to lead an invasion to unseat her father. What a dilemma: As she was legal heir, she said she would rule only if she and her husband could rule jointly. Parliament accepted her demand and by the end of the year her husband sent her father into exile. Meeting with both houses of Parliament in February 1689, William and Mary read the Declaration of Rights which would forever transform the rights of future sovereigns. Mary and her husband were crowned in April that year (Ascendant trine Saturn) and for the next five and a half years Mary kept pretty much to herself in the background. Two weeks before Christmas 1694, Mary fell ill and developed smallpox. William was terrified because both of his parents had died of this ailment. Mary II passed away on December 28, 1694 (Midheaven sesquisquare Sun, Ascendant square Neptune), leaving her husband William to rule alone.

Mary's life was quite traumatic due to her father's remarriage and conversion to Catholicism. She hid most of her feelings on matters of state and let her husband run the show. Physically, Mary was an imposing woman, standing 5'11", always majestic and regal in comportment. Her marriage produced no children; she was rumored to be a closet lesbian. Mary also had to deal with gossips who questioned her loyalty to her father for she was accused of snatching the throne for herself and her ambitious husband. Mary excelled at social gatherings due to her Aquarian Ascendant, which gave her the reputation of being selfless and serenely composed.

William III

William of Orange was born in The Hague, Netherlands on November 4, 1650 O.S. (November 14, 1650 N.S.) at 8:30 p.m. LAT (8:15 p.m. LMT), according to *William and Mary* by Van Der Zee. His father, William II of Orange, died a few months before his birth, shown by his natal Ascendant semisquare Pluto, ruler of his Sun sign. His mother, Mary, was sister to Charles II and died when

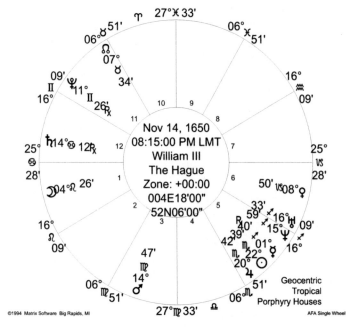

William was age 10 (progressed Midheaven square Venus). At age twenty-seven, he married his cousin Mary Stuart in November 1677 (Midheaven semisquare Pluto, ruler of the fifth house). Despite their initial difficulties, they soon learned to love each other and William grew quite dependent on a wife whom he adored.

William was crowned, along with his wife in April 1689 (Ascendant square Jupiter). With Mary's death in December 1694 (Ascendant sesquisquare Venus), William was devastated and disconsolate. He spent much time in prayer and began to drink heavily. He even broke off his long affair with Elizabeth Villiers. During the last years of his reign, the Bank of England was founded and the Civil List was instituted, giving the monarch a fixed income. In June 1701, the Act of Settlement stated the crown was to remain in Protestant hands even if it meant a foreign dynasty took over the throne.

William died on March 8, 1702 (progressed Midheaven opposite Jupiter, Ascendant semisquare Saturn), after suffering failing health for some years with asthma and rheumatism. William was respected but never really loved or admired by the English because he preferred his homeland to that of his wife. Like most Scorpios, William was reserved, suspicious, cold and impassive and seldom went out of his way for others. Physically, he was only 5'6" tall and rather gaunt with a large hooked nose. No wonder Mary cried at their wedding. On the battlefield, however, William was in his element with Aries on the Midheaven. He was cautious in speech, always taciturn and brusque. In love, William was bisexual and liked farm laborers, but only if they were Dutch. Despite the Moon in Leo, William had a reputation for being cold, hard and stingy, as well as very solemn.

Anne

Anne Stuart was born in London on February 6, 1655 O.S. (February 16, 1665 N.S.) at 11:39 p.m. LAT (11:54 p.m. LMT), according to a biography by David Green. Her mother, Anne Hyde, died when she was age six (Midheaven opposite Sun) and two years later her father remarried. Soon after, Anne met Sarah Churchill, later the Duchess of Marlborough (wife of the famous general) and formed a friendship that would last for many years. In July 1683,

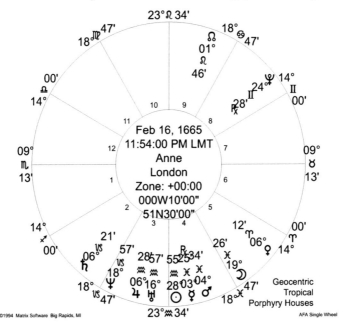

Feb 16, 1665
11:54:00 PM LMT
Anne
London
Zone: +00:00
000W10'00"
51N30'00"

Geocentric
Tropical
Porphyry Houses

©1994 Matrix Software Big Rapids, MI

AFA Single Wheel

137

Anne married Prince George, son of the King of Denmark, a dull man of few words who was trained as a soldier (Ascendant trine Moon). Since her sister had no children and English desperately needed a Protestant heir, during her marriage Anne became pregnant seventeen times. None of the children lived beyond infancy except the Duke of Gloucester, who survived only to age eleven. Anne's sister Mary died in 1694 of smallpox (Midheaven sesquisquare Jupiter, Ascendant square Sun), making Anne heir to the throne. In July 1700, Anne's only surviving child died and a year later her father James II died in France (Midheaven inconjunct Sun). Six months alter Anne became queen (Ascendant square Mercury) upon the death of her brother-in-law, with whom she had had a chilly relationship.

Anne came to the throne in poor health due to so many pregnancies. Her Ascendant ruler, Pluto, in the eighth house and square the Moon in her fifth house, was not a good omen for long lived offspring. Mars, co-ruler of her Ascendant, conjuncts Mercury, ruler of the eighth house. Despite that stubborn Scorpio Ascendant and Aquarian Sun, Anne refused to act independently and always sought advice from others; but that advice was often lacking in wisdom. Venus, ruler of her Descendant, squares Saturn, the planet of wisdom. During the early years of her reign, her friend Sarah Churchill's husband (the Duke of Marlborough) won one battle after another against the French. The Crown rewarded him by erecting Blenheim Palace where Winston Churchill was later born. In failing health, Anne left the running of government to others, paving the way for establishing the office of prime minister after her death.

In May 1707, the crowning glory of Anne's reign occurred when the Act of Union joined England and Scotland into a common unit. One year later, Anne's husband died of asthma (Midheaven opposite Venus square Saturn) and she gave up on life, sitting around the palace waiting to die. Her 30-year friendship with Sarah Churchill ended abruptly in 1710 when Sarah started spreading lies about the queen. It's said there was more than met the eye between them; some even said they were secret lovers, Anne being a closet lesbian like her sister. Broken and weary, Anne died on August 1, 1714 (progressed Sun square Neptune, Midheaven square Saturn-Neptune).

In many respects Anne should never have become queen. Having an isolated and unhappy childhood (Sun/Uranus midpoint opposing the Midheaven), she would have been content as a good wife and mother had history dealt her a different hand. Plain and fat in appearance, she was nearly six feet tall and her weight and husky frame made it increasingly difficult for her to walk because of bouts of rheumatism and gout. In perpetual pain, she was often moved about in a sedan chair or hoisted by pulleys. Mars rules her sixth house of health and is in Pisces, not a strong position for a planet of vitality. Temperamentally, she was weak and vacillating and, having never expected to sit on the throne, she was unprepared. Her physician said on her deathbed, "Sleep was never more welcome to the weary traveler than death was to her." Anne's demise left the monarchy in the hands of the Hanover dynasty from Germany, from whom the present queen is descended. Like the Tudors before her, the Stuart family passed into history without issue because they could not sire offspring who lived beyond infancy.

The Hanovers

George I

George, Prince of Brunswick-Luneberg, was born in Osnabruck, Germany on May 28, 1660 O.S. (June 7, 1660 N.S.) at 7:12 p.m. LAT (7:10 p.m. LMT) according to Martin Harvey's *Nativitas*. His father, Ernest August, was the Elector of Hanover; his mother, Sophia, was the daughter of Elizabeth, sister of Charles I. His predecessor, Queen Anne, was his second cousin.

George married the extremely attractive, vivacious, but flirtatious Sophia Dorothea of Celle (born September 15, 1666) in 1682 and their union produced two children (progressed Ascendant opposite Pluto). Seven year later, however, Sophia began an affair with the dashing Swedish Count von Konigsmarck which was to be her undoing. In July 1694, Konigsmarck was seen entering the palace in Hanover but was never seen coming out, leading to rumors that George, having discovered the affair, had his wife's lover murdered (Midheaven inconjunct Saturn). George then filed for divorce and Sophia was confined to a castle in Ahlden and forbidden to have any contact with her children (Ascendant inconjunct Venus sesquisquare Moon). George's Sun and Moon conjunction to Pluto made him quite vindictive and definitely not a person to be messed with. Four years later, upon the death of his father, George became Elector of Hanover (Midheaven square Mars).

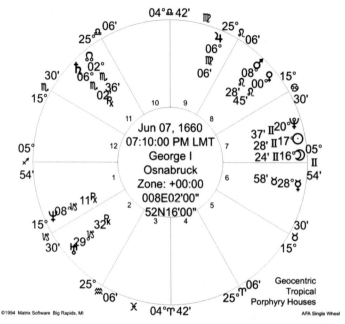

With the death of Queen Anne in 1714, George became King of England three months after the death of his mother (Ascendant inconjunct Pluto). George was quite unhappy at the prospect of having to leave his homeland and took his sweet time reaching England. His arrival caused quite a commotion for he brought with him two mistresses nicknamed the Elephant and the Maypole (so called because of their physiques) and two Turkish servants named Mustafa and Mahomet. George was not a striking figure of a man: He was of medium height, had large bulbous eyes, was stiff and formal in the German style, and spoke hardly a word of English. George conducted most of his meetings in French or German. George would have preferred to be left alone because his life in Hanover had been quiet an dull. Compared with previous English monarchs, he had no distinct style or flamboyance and was completely lacking in imagination. George spent as much time as possible in Hanover, about six months of the year if he was lucky.

One of his biggest worries revolved around James Francis Edward Stuart, the child of James II and his second wife. He was called the Pretender and his followers were called Jacobites; together they staged a rebellion in 1715 with the backing of King Louis XV of France. Fueled by hatred of the Act of Union, most of Scotland swore allegiance to the Stuart offspring. But the rebellion failed and a year later James III (as he was called in Scotland) fled to France. One of George I's biggest triumphs was in appointing Robert Walpole as his prime minister in 1722.

In November 1726, George's imprisoned wife died in her castle (Ascendant opposite Mars) and seven months later, on his way back to Hanover, George gorged himself at a banquet and passed out from an attack of diarrhea. He died June 11, 1727, in his hometown (Midheaven trine Mars), unlamented in the country he had ruled for the previous thirteen years. It's possible George simply didn't like the English way of life: His relocated Midheaven in London trined both Mercury and Uranus, and the relocated Ascendant trined Venus and sextiled Uranus and opposed Mercury. His frequent sojourns to his homeland and his open preference for anything German fueled dislike for this unhappy monarch.

Many thought his living openly with two mistresses while his wife was imprisoned was a bit extreme, but with George's luminaries conjunct Pluto, he was an all-or-nothing type of guy, no half-measures for him. The open conflicts with his son George II were legendary and their hatred for one another often placed Walpole in the middle, trying to reconcile father and son. Note that Mars rules George's fifth house and is semisquare Pluto and square Saturn. George would have preferred to completely ignore his son due to Mars inconjunct Neptune. George even considered having his son kidnapped and sent to America to get him out of his life once and for all.

George II

George II was born in Hanover, Germany on October 30, 1683 O.S. (November 9, 1683 N.S.) at 11:10 p.m. LAT (10:54 p.m. LMT) according to my rectification. With the exception of William the Conqueror and Henry II, this is the only speculative chart in this volume. Even Martin Harvey couldn't obtain a birth time as it was not mentioned on his birth registration. George was 11 when his mother was imprisoned for her affairs with that Swedish count (progressed Midheaven opposite Venus, Ascendant opposite Nep-

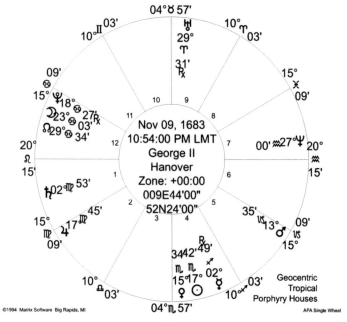

04°♉57'

10°♊03'

10°♈03'

29° ♈ 31' ♅ ℞

15° ♓ 09'

09'
⊗ 15° ♆ 18°
☽ 23° ⊗ 27℞
♌ 29° ⊗ 34' ℞
03'

20° ♌ 15'

Nov 09, 1683
10:54:00 PM LMT
George II
Hanover
Zone: +00:00
009E44'00"
52N24'00"

00' ♒ 27° ♆ 20°
♒ 15'

♄ 02 ♍ 53'

15° ♍ 09'
♃ 17 ♍ 45'

♒ 13° ♂ ♑ 09'
35'
15'

34 42' 49' ℞
♏ ♏ ♐
15° 17° 02°
♀ ☉ ☿
04° ♏ 57'

10° ♎ 03'

03' ♐ 10° 09'

Geocentric
Tropical
Porphyry Houses

©1994 Matrix Software Big Rapids, MI

AFA Single Wheel

tune). His father's treatment of his mother left a bitter taste in his mouth which led to open hostility between him and his father, who had forbidden George to see his mother ever again. Note that the Moon-Pluto conjunction in the twelfth house widely opposes Mars.

George II married Caroline of Ansbach (born March 1, 1683) in September 1705 (Midheaven square Neptune in the seventh house). It was one of the wisest moves he ever made because Caroline had all the virtues her husband lacked, such as patience and a sense of humor. George depended on her completely. In order for many political decisions to receive the monarch's approval, the ministers would first converse with Caroline, who would then butter up her husband. During George's frequent absences from England, Caroline would act as regent. She was so tolerant and obliging (typical of Pisces) that she chose his mistresses to make certain they were uglier than she was. Note that George II had Neptune in the seventh house and Uranus (ruler of the Descendant) sextiles that planet from the ninth house. Their union produced seven children. The English said she was "smart with the heart." But she could do little to quell the animosity between George and their eldest son,

Frederick, the Prince of Wales. For some reason, all the Hanovers seemed to detest their male offspring.

In November 1726, George's mother died in prison (Midheaven square Jupiter) and seven months later his father died while on a trip to his homeland (Ascendant inconjunct progressed Jupiter). Like his father, George II felt all things German were superior; he condemned fox hunting but loved music, especially anything composed by Handel, whom his father had made an English citizen. George kept his son Frederick in Hanover for more than a year and only reluctantly welcomed him to England. His son was given a small allowance so he couldn't become politically influential—Frederick was much more popular than his father. Notice that Mars in George's fifth house opposes Pluto but trines Jupiter for indications of his son's popularity and potential political threat.

In April 1736, Frederick married Princess Augusta of Saxe-Gotha, a big, gangly woman of seventeen who spoke not a word of English. Soon the couple was more popular than the king and queen. Frederick confronted Walpole for more money from the Civil List, much to the chagrin of his father. The couple kept Princess Augusta's pregnancy a secret so King George II wouldn't be looking over their shoulders, pulling the strings. When their firstborn entered the world in August 1737, the king and queen were furious, so Frederick and his wife were moved from St. James Palace to Kew. Frederick tried to apologize to his father, but George dismissed his son posthaste.

In November 1737, Queen Caroline died as the result of an umbilical infection incurred during childbirth (Midheaven sesquisquare Venus, Ascendant inconjunct Uranus). George was totally grief stricken and overwrought. On her deathbed, Caroline asked George to remarry. Frederick, however, was not even allowed into the chamber. Within a year, one of George's mistresses accidentally set fire to Kensington Place and within five years Walpole retired from his position of prime minister.

The Jacobites, who had first rebelled a year after George I became king, again tried to unseat the Hanovers. This time their leader was Bonnie Prince Charlie, son of the Stuart Pretender, a young lad of twenty-four. After initial successes in Scotland, the Highlanders marched south into England and after the bloodbath at

Culloden in 1746, they were forced to retreat. Bonnie Prince Charlie escaped to France dressed as a woman, thus ending the Jacobite dream once and for all. In March 1751, Frederick, the Prince of Wales, died of pleurisy at age 44 (Midheaven opposite Mars). Now his grandson, the future George III, would become the focus of the political opposition. George II died of a stroke while defecating at 7:13 a.m. on October 25, 1760 (Midheaven conjunct Moon, Ascendant square Pluto semisquare Saturn). George had suffered from constipation and piles for years due to the Sun in Scorpio and the Moon-Pluto conjunction in the twelfth house, not to mention Saturn rising.

Physically, George II was tall and well built with prominent, bulging blue eyes, ruddy skin, a large nose and a wide mouth. He loved uniforms due to the Ascendant occupying the Aries duad of Leo and was the last English monarch to lead his troops into battle at Dettington in 1743. George's temper was legendary and he often kicked his hat or wig around the room while screaming at full force. He was a martinet most of the time and everything had to be in its proper place, or else. Each night, George would wait outside the door of his mistress' apartment and at precisely 9:00 p.m. he would bang on her door and then go inside and complete his deed, often leaving his hat on while doing so. George didn't have the most polite manners and most considered him rude and vulgar. Always obstinate and pigheaded, he seldom yielded to anyone but his wife, whom he adored. When his reign ended, England was the largest empire on earth, the redcoats having established themselves firmly in India and Canada.

George III

George III was born in London on May 24, 1738 O.S. (June 4, 1783 N.S.), the second child of Frederick, the Prince of Wales (born January 20, 1707) and Princess Augusta. According to the biography *The King Who Lost America* by John Brooke, he was born between 6:00 and 7:00 a.m.; I've rectified the time to 6:45 a.m. LAT (6:43 a.m. LMT). Other biographies also give this time frame, but older references often have early Leo rising for this monarch.

George was a sickly child, born two months premature and not expected to survive his first year. Note the twelfth house planets op-

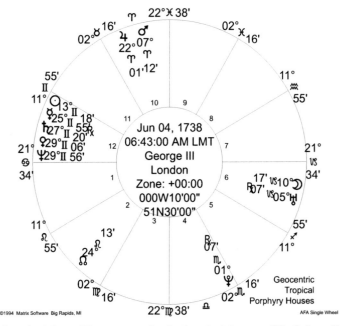

22°✕38'

02°✕16'

11° ≈ 55'

21° ♑ 34'

17' ♑ 10° ☽
♃07' ♑ 05° ⛢

55'

11° ♐

Geocentric
Tropical
Porphyry Houses

02° ♏ 16'

♇ 16'

♃ 07' ♏ 01°

22° ♍ 38' ♎

02° ♍ 16'

24° ♌ 8°

11° ♌ 55'

13'

02° ♋ 34'

21° ♋

♂ 29° ♊ 56'
♄ 29° ♊ 06'
♀ 27° ♊ 20' ℞
☿ 25° ♊ 18'
☉ 3° ♊

11° ♊

55' ♉

02° ♉ 16'

♃ ♂ 22° 07° ♈ ♈

01' 12'

22° ✕ 38'

Jun 04, 1738
06:43:00 AM LMT
George III
London
Zone: +00:00
000W10'00"
51N30'00"

10 9

11   8

12   7

1   6

2   5

3   4

©1994 Matrix Software Big Rapids, MI   AFA Single Wheel

posing the Moon-Uranus combo in the sixth house. His father died in March 1751 (progressed Midheaven square Uranus), leaving him heir to the throne. When his grandfather George II died in October 1760, George III began the longest reign in English history to that date (Midheaven sextile Sun, Ascendant inconjunct Uranus). One of his first official acts was to name Charlotte of Mecklenburg-Strelitz (born January 1744) as his bride, despite being madly in love with Hannah Lightfoot and wanting to marry Sarah Lennox. George and Charlotte's arranged union was happy and they grew to love each other in time. They produced fifteen children, nine sons and six daughters. Charlotte preferred quiet country living to the hustle and bustle of London. She was short and plain with a very large mouth, a trait seen in present day Hanovers like Princess Anne, who is also blessed with the oversized Hanover nose. George and Charlotte were crowned two weeks after their September 1761 marriage (Ascendant trine Mars).

In January 1765, George suffered a mysterious ailment with symptoms of sharp chest pains, coughing bouts, stomach spasms, wild seizures and general delirium, which interfered with his execution of royal duties for three months (Ascendant inconjunct Moon/Uranus midpoint). Doctors viewed George as going mad, unaware that he was afflicted with hepatic porphyria, inherited from his Stuart ancestor Mary Queen of Scots.

For the next five years, rebellion in the American colonies increased and war seemed imminent, especially after the 1773 Boston Tea Party. During the same period, George's mother died (Ascendant semisquare Venus-Saturn). After England lost the American colonies, George considered abdicating (Midheaven trine Uranus) and had numerous fights with Parliament and the prime minister. George's health continued to deteriorate. In a second bout with "insanity" in 1788 (Midheaven semisquare Mercury-Saturn, Ascendant sesquisquare Moon), his fits prompted him to talk incessantly and experience blurred vision. On one ride in Hyde Park, George halted the carriage to exit and converse with an oak tree, mistaking it for the King of Prussia. The Moon-Uranus conjunction in the sixth house didn't bode well for George's mental stability and with half the planets and luminaries positioned in the twelfth house (including Mercury, ruler of his Sun), the Neptunian delusions are clearly seen. Considering his frail constitution at birth, it's amazing that George lived as long as he did.

George had numerous problems with his sons. The Prince of Wales (later George IV) was a womanizer and gambler who created a flurry of scandalous rumors and widespread debt. His architectural extravagances surpassed the crown's wealth. His marriage to a Catholic widow shocked his countrymen. Another son (later William IV) shared a lengthy and reproductively fruitful affair with an actress. Still another son, the Duke of Kent (Queen Victoria's father), wreaked havoc in Canada with his affair and the mistreatment of troops in his command, which threatened to end in mutiny.

George III's reign did produce some good effects. Despite his losing America, colonization continued with the 1788 Australian settlement. English victories dominated wars with France against Napoleon. Heroic leadership like that of Nelson and Wellington earned British troops and sailors a reputation as a formidable force. Napoleon, the Little Corporal, was banished to faraway St. Helena and Europe eliminated its twenty year fear of the French army.

With the death of his youngest daughter in 1810 (Midheaven inconjunct Pluto, Ascendant trine Moon), George flew into a rage and was confined in a straightjacket because his violent outbursts had become a serious threat to his safety. Viewing his father's ailment as temporary but preventing current royal functioning, the Prince of Wales became regent. By summer 1811, a relapse rendered George incoherent; he refused to eat and was unable to sleep. Within three years he was totally senile and off in his own world. George III died at Windsor on January 29, 1820 (Ascendant semisquare Pluto).

George IV

George was born August 12, 1762 at 7:24 p.m. LAT (7:28 p.m. LMT) according to a biography by Christopher Hibbert. As a newborn he was put on display in drawing rooms and remained in the limelight (typical of Leo Sun conjunct Neptune). He matured early, able to speak in formal company by age two, but was kept in baby clothes by his father and sheltered from the outside world. After a brief scandal when an actress demanded cash for love letters he had written while in the throes of their affair, there was an unsuccessful effort to keep George IV on a tight rein. When he was 21, his residence at Carlton House became the center of London society (progressed Ascendant conjunct Uranus).

A secret 1785 marriage to Maria Fitzherbert, a widow six years his senior, threatened his position as heir to the throne. Not only was the marriage illegal and unsanctioned by the king, the bride was Catholic (Midheaven sesquisquare Neptune). Two years later George moved to Brighton in an effort to curb his extravagant spending (Uranus in the second house ruled by Mars in Scorpio opposite Moon-Jupiter). Instead, Brighton became *the* place to be (Midheaven trine Jupiter) and George's bills accounted for one-fourth of the annual royal budget. He even denounced the French Revolution in Parliament, positioning to acquire additional funds from English coffers. Finally, to cancel the massive debt, George agreed to wed his cousin, Caroline of Brunswick, after an annulment from Maria. George and Caroline married in April 1795 (Midheaven trine Moon, Ascendant conjunct Jupiter) and their wedding night tested the limits of belief. Physically re-

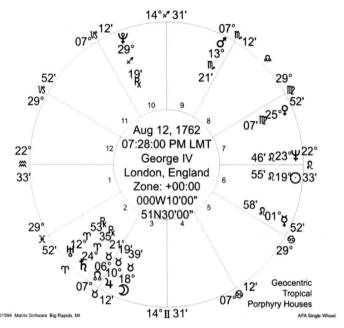

14°♐31'

07°♑12' ♆ 29° ♐ 19'℞

07°♏12' ♂ 13° ♏ 21'

52' ♑ 29°

07°♏25°♀ 29° ♍ 52'

22° ♒ 33'

Aug 12, 1762
07:28:00 PM LMT
George IV
London, England
Zone: +00:00
000W10'00"
51N30'00"

46' ♌23°♆ 22°♌
55' ♌19○33'

29° ♓ 52'

53'℞ ♂℞ 35' 12° ♈ 21'♉ 39' 24° ♉ 06°♉ 10° ♉18° 07°♉ ♃ ♉12' ☽

58' ♌01'☿ 52' ♋
29°

12' 07°♋

Geocentric
Tropical
Porphyry Houses

©1994 Matrix Software Big Rapids, MI

14°♊31'

AFA Single Wheel

pulsed by his bride, George got drunk and slept on the floor. He complained that Caroline (born May 17, 1768) was fat and dumpy; she reached 225 pounds at one point. Freed of debt, the monarchy needed an heir. George and Caroline spent only one night together, but nine months later Princess Charlotte was born. George and Caroline kept up appearances for a year, then went their separate ways. Her later behavior was often scandalous, disgraceful and indiscreet, while George returned to the good life in Brighton.

In November 1810 George IV became regent and took control of the government (Midheaven opposite Mercury). Three years later, George's wife, denied access to her daughter and ignored for the past 18 years by her husband, returned to Germany. Meanwhile, George spared no expense in his patronage of artists, musicians, sculptors and architects. His plan to link Carlton House with Regent's Park was a lasting contribution to English town planning. In November 1817, Princess Charlotte died in childbirth (Ascendant inconjunct Mars) and a year later George's mother died (Midheaven square Jupiter). Upon his father's death in January

1820, George became king (Midheaven sesquisquare Venus), a position he'd held unofficially for nine years.

The July 1821 coronation was the most lavish and costly England had ever witnessed. George's estranged wife, now Queen Caroline, was barred from the ceremony and died three weeks later, to the king's relief (Ascendant semisquare Mercury). George's lifestyle had caught up with him; he was seriously overweight and crippled by gout. Romance with a new partner in her fifties and with four children lightened his life for a bit. He died June 26, 1830 (Midheaven opposite Sun, Ascendant square Venus) penniless, as he had been for most of his adult life.

George was called the Prince of Pleasure and was tall and handsome in his youth, always charming and dignified. He had style and taste, and set fashion trends during the Regency period. Like most Leo types, he was a gambler and hated to be ignored. The Moon-Mars opposition made him sexually profligate, often immoral, always a libertine. The Mars-Jupiter opposition contributed to his flamboyance; he was a voluptuary and lived life to its fullest. Where food was concerned, he was a glutton and a gourmand. With his Aquarius Ascendant, he led the "royal rat pack" and got the lion's share of headlines as heir to the throne. His amorous liaisons can be traced to a Venus-Pluto square and Neptune in the seventh house. In contrast to the present royal family, George reveled in the continual publicity and limelight, and would have delighted in giving the tabloids a run for their money.

William IV

William, Duke of Clarence, was born in London on August 21, 1765 between 3:00 and 4:00 a.m. according to Fitzgerald's biography. I rectified the time to 3:35 LAT (3:38 LMT). Most of William's early life was in the Royal Navy, where he earned a reputation for salty language and cavorting with the ladies. His foreign journeys and love of adventure are exemplified by the Moon-Uranus opposition across the third-ninth houses. In 1790, William began an affair with actress Dorothea Jordan (progressed Midheaven trine Venus sesquisquare Pluto, progressed Ascendant conjunct Neptune), who bore him 10 illegitimate children surnamed Fitzclarence. William disinherited the children in 1811

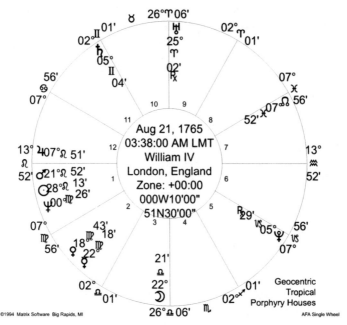

Chart wheel labels:

26°♈06'

♅ 25° ♈ 02'

02° ♈ 01'

02°♊01'

♄ 05° ♊ 04'

56' ♋ 07°

07° ♓ 56'

52'♓ 07°♌ 56'

13° ♌ 52' ♃07°♌51'
♂21°♌52'
☊28°♌13'
☿00♍26'

Aug 21, 1765
03:38:00 AM LMT
William IV
London, England
Zone: +00:00
000W10'00"
51N30'00"

13° ♒ 52'

07° ♍ 56'
♀18♍22'

♇29'

♇05°♑56'
07°

43'18'

21' ♎

02° ♎ 01'

22° ☽

02°♏ 01'

26°♎06' ♏

Geocentric
Tropical
Porphyry Houses

AFA Single Wheel

when he and Dorothea parted company (Midheaven semisquare Uranus). In the royal rush for heirs after Princess Charlotte's death, William married Adelaide of Saxe-Meiningen (born August 21, 1792) in July 1818. Adelaide was a plain, self-effacing woman with high moral standards. She tolerated her husband's previous offspring as her own two children died in infancy.

When George IV died in 1830, William inherited a nearly bankrupt monarchy. During his reign there were numerous reforms such as that which widened the voting franchise and redistributed seats in Parliament. Seriously stricken with asthma, William died June 20, 1837 (Midheaven opposite Pluto, Ascendant trine Saturn), leaving the throne to his niece Victoria.

Despite being a double Leo, William hated pomp and ceremony. Always direct, hearty and candid, he often appeared silly and with a weird sense of humor. Unlike other royals his age, William was unsophisticated and loved to mingle with crowds. His cheerful unaffected manner endeared him to his subject and during his brief reign he returned a sense of normalcy to the monarchy.

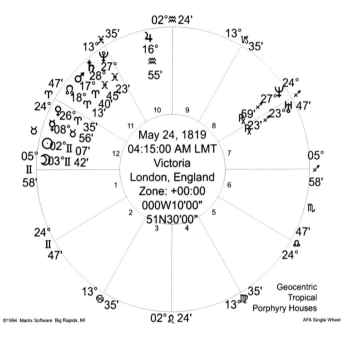

02°≈24'

13°♈35'
13°♓
♆
♄ 27°
28° ♓
♂ 17° ♓
♀ 18° ♈ 23'
47' ♈ 40' 45'
24° ♀ 26° 13'
☿ 08° ♉ 35'
♉ 56'
☊ 02° ♊ 07'
05° ☽ 03° ♊ 42'
♊
58'

♃
16°
≈
55'

13°♑35'

♅ 24°
♆ 27° ♐
♅ 23° ♐ 47'
♊ 59' ♐
℞ 23'
℞

10   9

11   8

May 24, 1819
04:15:00 AM LMT
12   7   05°
Victoria   ♐
London, England   58'
Zone: +00:00   ♏
1   000W10'00"
2   51N30'00"
3   4   5

6

24°
♊
47'

24°
♎
47'
05°
♐
58'
♏

24°

13°♋35'
♋

35' ♍
13°   Geocentric
02°♌24'   Tropical
Porphyry Houses

©1994 Matrix Software Big Rapids, MI   AFA Single Wheel

Victoria

She was born in Kensington Palace, London, on May 24, 1819 at 4:15 a.m. LMT according to a biography by Elizabeth Longford. Her father Edward, Duke of Kent (born November 2, 1767 at noon), was the third son of George III and died January 1820 when Victoria was less than a year old (progressed Midheaven trine Moon). Her mother, Victoria of Saxe-Leiningen, was thirty-one, the widow of the Prince of Leiningen and sister to King Leopold of Belgium. Bossy and pushy, Victoria's mother tried to keep her isolated from the ribald court of her uncles. When William took the throne in 1830, Victoria's mother and consort John Conroy (whom Victoria detested) conspired to make the elder Victoria regent. Mama Victoria constantly quarreled with the king about the heiress to the throne. Fortunately, the young Victoria's governess, Baroness Lehzen, prepared her well for her future role as queen.

Victoria became queen in June 1837 (Midheaven sextile Mars, Ascendant opposite Uranus), three weeks past her eighteenth birthday, and no longer needing her mother's regency. At 20, Victoria announced plans to marry her cousin, Prince Albert of Saxe-Coburg-Gotha (born August 26, 1819 at 6:00 a.m. in Rosenau). They were wed in February 1840 (Midheaven sextile Uranus, Ascendant opposite Neptune). Despite the image of the Victorian Age, Victoria was a romantic, in love with love, and definitely in love with her husband. From surviving diary accounts, they had a physically active union with Victoria complaining that her husband was too passive, although they had nine children in 18 years.

Victoria hated being pregnant because it spoiled the romantic side of her life with Albert, but she kept her mouth shut in public about what she considered an inconvenience. Much to her dismay, Albert had no official title until "Prince Consort" was proposed shortly before the birth of their last child. Victoria and Albert traveled from one royal retreat to another, their favorite being Osborne House on the Isle of Wight. They spent summers in Scotland at Balmoral Castle, which Albert completely redecorated.

Due to the fortunate marriages of her children to members of various royal families, Victoria became known as "the grandmother of Europe." Her eldest daughter, Vicky, married Frederick, Crown Prince of Germany, and produced Kaiser Wilhelm II. Another daughter married the Duke of Hesse and produced Princess Alix, later Tsarina of Russia and wife to Nicholas II. Another granddaughter was mother to (the current) Prince Philip.

Victoria had strained relations with all her prime ministers except Lord Melbourne, whom she idolized as a father figure. Her battle of wills with Gladstone and Disraeli were legendary. Victoria's meeting with Napoleon III in Paris was historic as the first time an English monarch had trod French soil without aim of conquest.

Victoria's mother died in March 1861 at age seventy-four (Midheaven semisquare Venus). The same year, Prince Edward returned from a triumphant American tour and became embroiled in a seedy sex scandal. Albert was outraged and his frail health weakened even more. Albert died of typhoid fever on December 14, 1861 and Victoria blamed her son for her husband's death. She entered a prolonged period of mourning, wore only black and seldom appeared in public. She even held seances, trying to contact the spirit of her dead husband. When John Brown, a Balmoral servant, became her constant companion, tongues began to wag. Brown was six years her junior, and many thought he and the queen were lovers and referred to her as "Mrs. Brown." Victoria ignored all this.

In 1861, India was turned over to the Crown, thereby enlarging the British Empire. In 1877, Victoria was made Empress of India (Ascendant conjunct Uranus), a title she had coveted for years. No longer disdained by her upstart German relatives, she became Her Imperial Majesty. In 1887, her Golden Jubilee brought her out of retirement and was attended by more than 50 monarchs.

With Edward's birth in 1894, there were three direct heirs to the throne, a situation unequaled to date. Victoria's jubilee in 1897 renewed public affection for her; she had by then the longest reign in English history. Her health rapidly failed, plagued by indigestion, increased tiredness, worsening eyesight and sleep problems. Victoria died on January 22, 1901 (Midheaven semisquare Moon, Ascendant square mercury) at age 81, having ruled England for nearly 64 years.

Despite being a triple Gemini, Victoria could be a petty domestic tyrant. Her Gemini youthfulness occasionally erupted when she became overemotional and totally illogical. Despite her small stature (4'8") she commanded universal respect. Always forceful with the Sun rising, she could also be stiff and obdurate with Mercury in Taurus, and often strict and judgmental toward her children. The rampant flirtations of her youth gave way to compulsive hero-worship of her husband. After his death, she paraded her grief and met severe criticism for avoiding public life. Victoria's inner woman (shown by Sun and Moon in the twelfth house) contrasted sharply with her public image. The impression we have of the Victorian Age as being stuffy, prim and proper was quite the opposite of the inner nature of the woman who gave her name to the era. Indeed, she was proud, vain and haughty, but not insufferably so, and she always presented herself in a regal manner. Despite her widely repeated statement, "We are not amused," she is said to have had a good sense of humor, somewhat adolescent in content. She seldom minced words, was honest and direct, but could come across as cold as iron if it suited her purpose.

As represented by Jupiter in her tenth house, the Victorian Age was one of wealth, opulence and expansion. By the time of Victoria's death, England ruled Canada, Australia, India and numerous small possessions, and was the largest empire on earth. Her four twelfth house planets point to an early life isolated from court activities. Her mother (shown by ruler of the IC, the Sun) was overly protective, overpowering and domineering. The early death of her father is shown by the ruler of the Midheaven (Uranus) close to the eighth house cusp and squaring Saturn and Pluto. The adoration and hero-worship of her husband is shown by Jupiter, ruler of the Descendant, sitting at the top of her chart and sextile Mars. Venus in the twelfth in Aries trines Uranus and Neptune, strong aspects for romanticism and having a "knight in shining armor." Despite the antics of her eldest son, Edward, Victoria managed to restore dignity and respect to the monarchy. Only a person with both luminaries conjunct the Ascendant could have put so personal a stamp on an historical age.

Edward VII

Edward, or Bertie as he was known to his family, was born in London on November 9, 1841 at 10:48 a.m. LMT, per his mother's diary. In temperament, he was the complete opposite of his father, Prince Albert, who was quite straitlaced and puritanical. He was more like his mother Victoria, being a romantic at heart and a *bon vivant*. Edward constantly embarrassed his parents to no end in his rebellion against a strict upbringing. Edward was restive, resentful and often vindictive, like most Scorpio types. He made a career in his youth of going against what he considered useless convention due to the Moon-Uranus opposition squaring his Ascendant. Some of his friends thought him slightly cruel because of the Moon square Saturn, which also made relations with his mother strained at times. Saturn rising made his life one of delayed responsibility due to its semisquare to the Sun. The many scandals in Edward's life could be due to his Sun square Neptune, which was also inconjunct Pluto. But the Sun trine Uranus made him the black sheep of the royal family, a profligate who lived life to its fullest due to Jupiter rising above the Ascendant.

Edward's father died of typhoid in December 1861 (progressed Ascendant sextile Sun) and, because of a scandal that had erupted earlier that year, he was blamed by his mother for her husband's un-

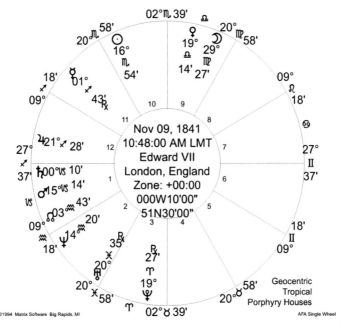

Chart details within the wheel:

02°♏39' ♎

20°♏58' ☉ 16° ♏ 54'

♀ 19° ♎ 14' ☽ 20°♍58' 29° ♍ 27'

18' ☿01° ♐
09°♐ 43'℞

09° ♌ 18'

♋

Nov 09, 1841
10:48:00 AM LMT
Edward VII
London, England
Zone: +00:00
000W10'00"
51N30'00"

27° ♐ 37' ♃21°♐ 28' ♄00°♑10' ♂15°♑14' ♎03°♒43' 20' ♆4°♓ ♇

27° Ⅱ 37'

18' Ⅱ 09°

09°♒ 18'

35°℞ 27°℞

20° ♐ 58' 20° ♐ 19° ♆ ♇ ♓ 02°♉39'

20°♉58'

Geocentric
Tropical
Porphyry Houses

timely demise. Victoria sought to marry off Edward as soon as possible in an effort to temper his freewheeling forays into the netherworld of society. A suitable princess was found in Alexandra (born December 1, 1844 at 7:00 a.m.), daughter of the King of Denmark. They married in March 1863 and produced five children. Alexandra was remarkable, for a less tolerant, more common woman (such as Princess Diana) would have chafed and bridled at her husband's indiscretions. Alexandra believed in granting her husband and children the maximum amount of freedom possible, so typical of a Sagittarius woman. Always dignified in public, she was greatly admired by the British for whom she always had a ready smile. Alexandra loved jewels and small animals and involved herself with many charitable works. She put up with her husband's many affairs because she knew that in his heart he loved her the most. And because she was deaf, and shy as a result, she was happy to forego many social occasions and remain in the background. Alexandra's Midheaven was conjunct Edward's Moon and his Sun sat on her Ascendant. Her Sun sat on Edwards's Ascendant and her Moon trined his Jupiter. Edward's last great affair, which endured for 10 years, was with Alice Keppel. Mrs. Keppel was warm, charming and discreet, which endeared her to everyone, including Princess Alexandra. When her husband was on his deathbed, Alexandra graciously summoned Mrs. Keppel to his bedside so she could say her final farewell. Incidentally, Alice Keppel's great-granddaughter is none other than Camilla Parker-Bowles, the notorious light-o'-love of Prince Charles.

Despite his strong marriage, which was a real love match, Edward continued to live the good life. In 1870 he was called into court to testify in a divorce case with a woman he had known since childhood (Midheaven conjunct Mercury). It created quite a scandal because no royal family member had been subpoenaed since the days of Henry IV. Edward was found not guilty but was vilified and harangued by the press. The next year Edward faced the threat of blackmail from a widow with whom he'd had a relationship years before and was forced to buy back love letters he had written her. Because of these scandals, Victoria refused suggestions from her prime minister that Edward be given some measure of responsibility in state affairs. Growing bored with life at home, Edward was sent to India in 1877 and was warmly received. Back at home, he was becoming quite the fashion plate, setting trends such as wearing a Homburg hat and a Norfolk jacket, and leaving the bottom button of his dinner jacket undone.

Edward had a fondness for theater people. His involvement with actress Lily Langtry caused few raised eyebrows because their affair occasioned no complaints from either Edward's wife or Lily's husband. Edward once boasted that he'd had more than 10,000 sexual conquests in his life, which works out to about four per week. He loved the egalitarian attitudes of France and America more than he did the stuffy, conservative class system of his native land. In 1884, Edward and Alexandra were granted a state income for life, thus alleviating the severe drain on their finances from attending functions his mother would normally do (Midheaven sextile Venus). Meanwhile, Victoria was still complaining that Edward was doing nothing but living the life of pleasure, but she obstinately refused to let Edward see any state papers.

In 1891, another scandal erupted, this one over a game of baccarat in which a buddy of Edward's was accused of cheating

(Midheaven conjunct Jupiter). The fact that the game was illegal made the public indignant—some example for the Prince of Wales to follow! The jury rejected the case, but soon after Edward was involved in another blackmail case, whereby a friend's mistress threatened to expose the private life of the prince. Finally, in 1892, Victoria agreed to let Edward see state papers for the first time (he was then 50) and before long Edward was entrenched in a commission to investigate the plight of the aged poor. In 1898, Edward took charge of the Privy Council (Midheaven conjunct Saturn), his first real position of responsibility and authority.

In late 1901, Queen Victoria died, leaving the throne to Edward, then age fifty-nine (Midheaven semisquare Sun). He stated that he wished to be known as Edward VII, not Albert I, as his mother would have preferred. His coronation, originally scheduled for June 26, 1902, had to be postponed because he suffered at attack of appendicitis for two and a half months. Edward's reign was like a breath of fresh air, letting out all the stuffiness of his mother's reign once and for all. The first state ball in more than six decades was held, and evening courts were introduced for the first time. Edward completely redecorated Buckingham Palace, which his mother had not used in years.

Edward became known as the Peacemaker after the Entente Cordiale was signed with France in 1904. He also made amends with his militant cousin Kaiser Wilhelm II, whose warlike ambitions were looming larger with each passing year. Edward visited Russia in 1908 to seal the Triple Entente, which placed England, France and Russia on a united course against German militarism. Edward died on May 6, 1910 (Ascendant trine Saturn inconjunct Moon), signaling the end of the Edwardian Era or La Belle Epoque. His funeral was attended by nine kings, seven queens and seventy ambassadors from all over Europe. In a manner of speaking, it was royalty's final showdown, for within a decade most of the mourners would be without jobs.

Edward's Sagittarius Ascendant indicated a life of pleasure, adventure and variety, doubly so because its ruler, Jupiter, rises just above the Ascendant. His love of fashion is shown by the Moon in Virgo and Venus in Libra at the top of his chart. Like most Sagittarius types, Edward was warm, spontaneous and enthusiastic, and was ironically known for tact and diplomacy later in life. Edward had a genuine concern for others, especially the less fortunate. He lived the good life, was a gourmet, smoked prodigiously, drank quite a bit, often gambled too much, and wooed the ladies with abandon. England loved him and he returned the favor.

House of Windsor

George V

George, second son of Edward and Alexandra, was born in London on June 3, 1865 at 1:30 a.m. LMT according to Victoria's diary. He grew up in the shadow of his elder brother Edward, Prince of Wales (aka Duke of Clarence), a dull and slow-witted kid who was dyslexic and partially deaf. Edward lacked initiative and was easily influenced by others; he had a reputation for folly and vice. There were rumors that Edward frequented gay brothels where he might have caught syphilis. Nevertheless, George dearly loved his elder brother and they took a two-year cruise around the world in 1881 (progressed Midheaven trined Mercury). George was trained as a naval officer where he garnered a reputation for being neat, orderly and punctual. In December 1891, Edward became engaged to Princess May, a cousin of Queen Victoria. Five weeks later, however, Edward was dead of pneumonia (progressed Ascendant trine Moon). The couple was to have wed in mid-February, but as George was now heir to throne, within four months he proposed to his dead brother's fiancé.

George and Mary (as she would henceforth be known) were married in July 1893 (Midheaven trine Moon). His bride was born in London on May 26, 1867, the granddaughter of the Duke of Wurttemburg who was married to a Hungarian countess. Mary had

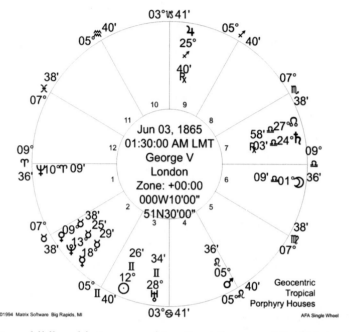

03°♑41'
05°♒40'
♃ 25° ✗
40' ℞
05° ✗ 40'

38'
♓
07°
07° ♏ 38'

10   9

11   8
Jun 03, 1865   58' ♎27°♌
01:30:00 AM LMT   ℞03' ♎24°♄
George V   7
London
Zone: +00:00   09°
000W10'00"   ♎
51N30'00"   09' ♎01°☽ 36'

09°
♈
36' ♇10°♈09'
12

1

2
3   4   5
6

07°
♉
38' ♀09°♉25'
♆13°♉29'
♂18°♉
☿8°
♍
38'
07°

26'   34'
♊
12°   ♊
28°
♅   36°
♌
05°
♂ 40'
05°♌

05°
♊ 40'   ☉
03°♋41'

Geocentric
Tropical
Porphyry Houses

©1994 Matrix Software Big Rapids, MI   AFA Single Wheel

a poor childhood but managed to attract the eye of the Prince of
Wales due to her connections at court. Like many with Aquarius
rising, Mary had little interest in sex per se and took little interest in
her children. She was always dignified in public—proud and
stately and rather old fashioned in her choice of attire, especially in
later years. She was very self-controlled but possessed of an in-
domitable spirit. The press kept silent about her one chief fault: The
Queen of England was a kleptomaniac. Her marriage to George
was one of convenience, however they did produce six children.
Her death in 1953 was hastened as Mary did not want the planned
coronation of her granddaughter Elizabeth II to be postponed due to
the official period of mourning. Some say she was poisoned to has-
ten her last breath; her son Edward, Prince of Wales, knew of the
plan as he was there when she passed away. True to her sense of
duty, she did not want to interfere with plans already underway.
Churchill once said of her, "She looked like a queen and acted like a
queen."

With the death of Queen Victoria in 1901, Edward VII became
king (progressed Ascendant conjunct Sun). Nine years later

162

George was on the throne (progressed Midheaven sesquiquadrate Moon and progressed Ascendant semisquare Mars). Journeying to India in 1911, Edward laid the cornerstone for the city of New Delhi. The gravest crisis to hit Europe in a century erupted in late June 1914 when the Archduke Franz Ferdinand, heir to the throne of Austria-Hungary, was shot by a Serbian anarchist in Sarajevo. Soon, drums of war were beating across the continent and England declared war on Germany during the first week of August (Ascendant opposite Jupiter). While inspecting the Royal Flying Corps (RFC) in France in October 1915, George was thrown from his horse, cracking a few ribs and fracturing his pelvis (progressed Ascendant conjunct Uranus).

To hide the German origins of the royal family, the House of Hanover became the House of Windsor in May 1917. After the unfortunate abdication of his cousin Tsar Nicholas II of Russia (who looked as if he were a twin brother of George), the British refused to grant the Russian royal family safe haven in England, bowing to pressure from Parliament, which considered Nicholas a tyrant.

George was devastated by the death of his mother in November 1925 (progressed Midheaven inconjunct Moon) whom he worshiped and adored. An emergency operation in late 1928 took place when George slipped into unconsciousness after a bout with pneumonia.

George celebrated his jubilee in 1935 after a quarter of a century on the throne—a period fraught with tension due to World War I and the Great Depression. During the depression of the 1930s, the royal family took a 50,000 pound pay cut as strikes and demonstrations across England were ominous (progressed Midheaven inconjunct Mars and progressed Ascendant square Neptune). George was surprised by the affection the British had for him as he always maintained he was just an ordinary fellow. George died on January 20, 1936 at 11:55 p.m. Some said his demise was planned in order to make the morning papers and he was given drugs to ease the pain of bronchial catarrh (progressed Midheaven square Sun and progressed Ascendant sextile Pluto).

George's main interests were yachting and philately. He was a short man (5'5") with a snub nose and a booming voice, a man of simplicity and integrity. Being a conservative at heart, he feared changed more than anything. Despite his aloof and distant manner, he endeared himself to his people and, in political matters, used plain, common sense and displayed an excellent grasp of details. The most remarkable thing about his reign is that, despite the turmoil of the world around him, George maintained his position—unlike many of his relatives who lost their thrones and went into exile or were assassinated. George was private and not ostentatious, a man with a strong sense of duty. He sought moderation in all things, being true to his Moon in Libra.

Edward VIII

Edward was born at White Lodge in Richmond, Surrey, England on June 23, 1894 at 9:55 p.m. GMT according to The London Times. In 1907 Edward entered the Royal Naval College—a bit of a mystery seeing as how this would prepare him for a career he could never use (progressed Ascendant square Venus). Edward's father became king in 1910 (progressed Midheaven sextile Saturn opposite Jupiter; progressed Ascendant trine Sun) which catapulted this schoolboy into the spotlight from which he would seldom escape until his death. Two years after his father's coronation, he enrolled in Magdalen College at Oxford and began to set the style of informality for which he was so famous. By the end of 1914, Edward was on the front lines in France (progressed Ascendant trine Uranus).

After the war, the Prince of Wales made the first of his many world tours. His love affair with America and Canada began in 1919 when he proclaimed he was rapidly becoming a westerner. After returning home to England for a while, Edward spent six months in Australia and New Zealand. During the 1920s, Edward's love interest was a married woman, Freda Dudley Ward, with two children. In 1931, one of Edward's friends, Lady Furness, introduced him to Mr. and Mrs. Ernest Simpson (progressed Midheaven sesquiquadrate Venus). Three years later Edward stopping seeing Freda and Lady Furness and had eyes only for Mrs. Simpson, nee Wallis Warfield, a divorcee from Baltimore whose husband was more than understanding and permissive of his wife's attraction to the Prince of Wales. Before long, Edward and Wallis were taking holidays together, although their relationship was kept hidden from

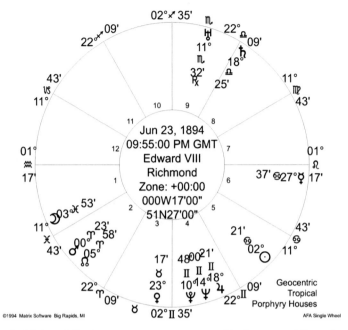

02°♐35'

22°♐09'

02°♐35' ♏
♅
11°
♏
32'
℞
25'

22°♎09'
♄
18°
♎

11°♍
43'

43'
♑
11°

01°
♒
17'

Jun 23, 1894
09:55:00 PM GMT
Edward VIII
Richmond
Zone: +00:00
000W17'00"
51N27'00"

01°
♌
17'

37' ♋27°☿

03°♐53'

11°
♓
43'

♂00°♈
05°

23'
58'

17' 48°00♉21'

21'
♅
02°♋

43'
♋
11°

02°♋
☉

22°♈09'

23°
♀

♉

II II II
10♂14♂18°
♆ ♃
02°Ⅱ35'

22°Ⅱ09'

Geocentric
Tropical
Porphyry Houses

©1994 Matrix Software Big Rapids, MI

AFA Single Wheel

the British public due to an arrangement with the press. Times have changed!

In January 1936, Edward became king upon the death of his father (progressed Midheaven inconjunct Neptune; progressed Ascendant sextile Sun semisquare Jupiter). He was the first bachelor to ascend the throne since William II. On his deathbed George V said, "After I am gone, the boy will ruin himself in twelve months." Edward was bored with the responsibilities which he now faced. He let state papers pile up, was quite late for appointments and behaved inconsiderately. Edward's relationship with the German ambassador, von Ribbentrop, caused considerable concern as von Ribbentrop's pro-Nazi sympathies were well known. During that fateful summer of 1936, Edward openly showed his affection for Wallis Simpson, which led to speculation that he planned to marry her. In October, Wallis filed for divorce from Ernest Simpson on grounds of adultery. Within the month Edward informed his family he intended to marry this American divorcee and thereby set into motion a constitutional crisis. Prime Minister Stanley Baldwin said Parliament would never accept Wallis Simpson as his consort, to which Edward replied he would abdicate if necessary. Queen Mary was livid, as was Edward's brother, the Duke of York (George VI) and his wife Elizabeth.

Three proposals were considered: First, Edward would marry Wallis and she would become queen; second, Edward and Wallis would marry, but she would not become queen and their union would be morganatic (Ed. note: A morganatic marriage is one where a member of a royal family is married to a person of non-royal lineage and in which the spouse and any offspring do not acquire, inherit or succeed to the titles, fiefs or entailed property of the parent of royal lineage; a form of marriage popular among European royalty when marrying a person without rank of nobility.); and, third, Edward would abdicate and the Duke of York would become king. Edward favored the second choice which included, in this case, making his wife a duchess, but leaving their children without rights of succession. On December 3, 1936, Wallis fled England for the south of France, stating she would step out of the picture if it meant Edward had to abdicate. Churchill and Lord Beaverbrook tried to rally support for the king, but Parliament, the cabinet and dominion leaders were against any marriage between Edward and Wallis. Edward made his decision December 8, 1936 and two days later signed the instrument of abdication. The next night over radio, Edward announced for the world to hear, "I have for 25 years tried to serve, but you must believe me when I tell you that I have found it impossible to carry the heavy burden of responsibility and to discharge my duties as king as I would wish to do without the help and support of the woman I love." On December 12, 1936, the king who was never crowned and the first monarch in English history to voluntarily abdicate, sailed for France to be with his beloved. On June 3, 1937, Edward and Wallis, now the Duke and Duchess of Windsor, were married at the Chateau de Cande near Tours. It has been reported that Edward was much dismayed that Wallis would never be known as Her Royal Highness.

For the remainder of their lives, the Windsors moved from one place to another. In August 1940, the Duke was appointed governor general of the Bahamas (progressed Midheaven square Saturn inconjunct Jupiter), a position which Parliament thought would keep him beyond the reach of Nazi sympathizers. After the war the couple alternated between New York and Paris, thus becoming the darlings of high society and the emerging jet set. On May 28, 1972, the Duke of Windsor died in Paris (progressed Midheaven trine Jupiter and Saturn); a week later he was buried at Frogmore. Queen Elizabeth visited her favorite uncle two weeks before his death and tried to make amends with the duchess after years of indifference. The duchess died in Paris on April 24, 1986 at age 91. At her funeral, Queen Mother Elizabeth finally buried the hatchet for the woman she had accused of bringing on the premature death of her husband, George VI, who had assumed the royal duties Edward neglected.

The Moon in Edward's first house indicated the numerous travels he undertook for the crown during his tenure as Prince of Wales. He was the consummate goodwill ambassador for the Commonwealth and those travels assuaged his continual restlessness shown by the square of the natal Moon to the Midheaven. Note also that the ruler of the Ascendant (Uranus) occupies the ninth house of foreign travel. Edward's temperament was more American than British; he hated useless rituals, outdated ceremonies and frivolous displays of pomp—all typical of Aquarius rising. Edward, being democratic at heart, sincerely had the welfare of his people at heart; however, his Cancer Sun in the fifth house squared by Mars in Aries in the second house eventually contributed to his final downfall. Note, again, that Uranus (ruler of the Ascendant) inconjuncts both Neptune and Pluto in the fourth house, pointing to the rift within his family caused by his unusual marriage.

Edward was youthful and charming, of slight build and modest height (5'6") with fair hair. A shy and nervous man, he needed solitude to escape the pressures of royal life. His principle fault was falling in love with an older woman. There are some who believe he was a closet homosexual; he was alleged to have had problems with premature ejaculation. After Edward met Wallis, such gossip seemed to fade away—perhaps because Wallis supposedly had spent time in Hong Kong, rumored to be in a Chinese brothel, learning the art and techniques of promoting sexual satisfaction.

Wallis Warfield was born in Baltimore, Maryland on June 19, 1895 according to the biography by Charles Higham. Her birth year was altered because her parents were not married when she was conceived and her mother had spent the last months of the pregnancy in the mountains outside Baltimore to escape the eyes of the press. Her father died of tuberculosis shortly after she was born. Wallis' first marriage was in 1920 to Earl Spencer, a United States naval officer who allegedly was prone to alcoholism. They divorced in 1927 and, the following year, Wallis married Ernest Simpson. Two years later, the Simpsons moved to England and, as is said, the rest is history.

George VI

Prince Albert, as he was christened, was born at Sandringham House in Norfolk on December 14, 1895 at 3:05 a.m. GMT according to *Sabian Symbols* by Marc E. Jones. Some biographies give the time as 3:10 a.m. and George V's diary mentions the time as 3:45 a.m. Since all clocks at Sandringham reportedly were kept 30 minutes fast, the earlier time may be appropriate. In 1909, Albert was enrolled at the Royal Naval College. This was one year before his father became king (progressed Midheaven square Uranus). The prince, however, had a predisposition to seasickness—not good for a naval cadet. In childhood Albert was continually in poor health, having persistent gastric troubles and wearing leg braces. During World War I he transferred from the navy to the Royal Air Force (progressed Midheaven square Mars).

In June 1920 George met Lady Elizabeth Bowes-Lyon (born August 4, 1900), daughter of the Earl of Strathmore. Three years later in April 1923, they were married. It was a love match from the beginning; Elizabeth's Sun was conjunct Albert's Midheaven and both their Moons were in Scorpio. Unlike previous royal brides, the new Duchess of York was not only a commoner but a full-blooded Englishwoman—the first since James II married Anne Hyde two and a half centuries earlier. When Elizabeth was a little girl, a gypsy fortune teller told her one day she would be queen. Her husband, oddly enough, told her the same thing. The Queen Mother was the most beloved and popular of the royals—a charming woman who smiled a lot and managed to radiate serenity seldom found in public figures. Always a fashion statement (she was known for her hats), she was a tower of strength for her husband and together they shared the same inconveniences and burdens as did the common

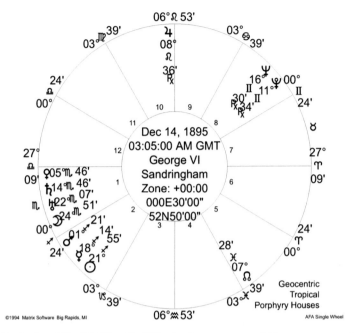

Dec 14, 1895
03:05:00 AM GMT
George VI
Sandringham
Zone: +00:00
000E30'00"
52N50'00"

Geocentric
Tropical
Porphyry Houses

©1994 Matrix Software Big Rapids, MI

AFA Single Wheel

folk during World War II. Elizabeth encouraged George to work with a speech therapist to eliminate his stammering in the fall of 1926 (progressed Ascendant conjunct Moon/Saturn midpoint.

The year 1936 began with the death of George's father (progressed Midheaven square Sun) and ended with George becoming king upon the abdication of his brother (progressed Midheaven sextile Uranus semisquare Jupiter). Due to his frail physical condition, people wondered if George would be up to the tremendous responsibilities a monarch must endure. However, what George lacked in physical strength, he clearly made up in determination. A man of steady virtues like solidity and reliability, he accomplished much more than originally expected. In the summer of 1939, the king and queen visited Canada and the United States—the first time a reigning monarch had set foot in the New World (progressed Midheaven sextile Moon and semisquare Jupiter). Huge crowds greeted the couple in Washington where they were warmly received by the Roosevelts. Soon after they returned to England, Hitler invaded Poland, beginning World War II. George and his family narrowly escaped death in September 1940 when Buckingham Palace was bombed by the Germans. To demonstrate their solidarity and to serve as an example to the British people, the royal family stayed in London during the Blitz rather than escaping to the country or to another land. It was an act the British would never forget. In August 1942, George's brother, the Duke of Kent, was killed in a flying accident (progressed Ascendant semisquare Saturn), bringing the horror of war into the palace. To cut back on the amount of imported food, the royal family plowed up their park at Windsor Castle and planted their own victory garden. Economy also drove them to turn down the heat in the palace and they rationed supplies as did the rest of England. Ten days after the allies landed at Normandy Beach on June 6, 1944, George inspected his troops at the front; and four months later he met with Field Marshall Montgomery in The Netherlands (progressed Ascendant conjunct Mars). After the war in Europe ended in May 1945, Buckingham Palace was the focal point of victory celebrations.

But soon after the war ended, England's vast empire started to crumble. No longer was George the Emperor of India after that region was granted its freedom in August 1947 (progressed Midheaven sextile Mars). In early 1949, an operation to restore circulation in his right leg was necessary as arteriosclerosis caused by heavy smoking threatened gangrene or amputation. Lung cancer was diagnosed in mid-1951 and on February 6, 1952, George VI passed away in his sleep (progressed Ascendant trine Jupiter).

Despite his lack of preparation for being a monarch, George rose to his position with dignity and resolve due to his Moon in Scorpio. George was far tougher than his detractors imagined and his strong sense of duty and innate decency endeared him to his people. Always formal and very concerned with appearances due to his Libra Ascendant, he restored a monarchy disgraced by his brother's abdication. George's physical problems are shown by Jupiter (ruler of his Sun sign) square Venus (ruler of the Ascendant). The Sun opposite Neptune also contributed to his frailty; but, with Jupiter at the Midheaven, one could have predicted prominence and glory for this man who was not born to be king.

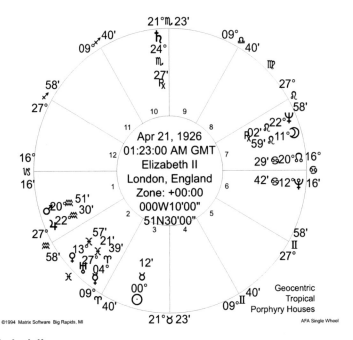

21°♏23'

ħ
24°
♏
27'
Ŗ

09°♐40'

09°♎40'

58'
♐
27°

♍
27°
♌
58'

Apr 21, 1926
01:23:00 AM GMT
Elizabeth II
London, England
Zone: +00:00
000W10'00"
51N30'00"

R 02' ♌ 22°Ψ
59' ♌ 11°☽

16°
♒
16'

29' ♋20°♌ 16°
♋
42' ♋12°Ψ 16'

27°
♒
58'

II
58'
♋
27°

20°♒51'
♂ 30'
22°♒

13°♓21'
♀27°♓39'
♅04°♈
♇

57'

12'

♈
09°
40'

☉
00°

♉
00°

09°♊40'

Geocentric
Tropical
Porphyry Houses

©1994 Matrix Software Big Rapids, MI

21°♉23'

AFA Single Wheel

Elizabeth II

Princess Elizabeth, elder daughter of the Duke and Duchess of York, was born at 21 Bruton Street in the Mayfair section of London on April 21, 1926. *The London Times* reported she came into the world at 2:40 a.m. BST, but this reported time has never worked for me. When I saw a pamphlet by Angela Gallo entitled *Celebrity Horoscopes*, I noticed she used the time of 2:23 a.m. BST—17 minutes earlier than the supposedly accurate birth time. Whether this time was a rectified one or whether Ms. Gallo had some inside information, it worked perfectly for me also. For those readers who require A or AA data and cast aside all others, please read further.

When Elizabeth was introduced to Wallis Simpson shortly before her uncle's abdication in 1936, she asked, "Who is she?" the reply was, "She is the woman who will put the crown of England on your head and the burden of being a constitutional monarch on your shoulders." Few could have predicted such an outcome at her birth, but a similar prediction was made at the birth of her sister Margaret when an astrologer noted a future domestic crisis when Margaret reached six years of age. The British had nothing against Americans, per se; only that Wallis Simpson was twice divorced and, consequently, unable to become queen. Elizabeth does have American connections from her mother's side of the family: Her eighth grandfather was Colonel Augustine Warner, who happened to be George Washington's great-grandfather. With the abdication of her uncle, Edward VIII, her father, the Duke of York, became King of England, a role for which he was unprepared (progressed Ascendant square Sun). Four days after Elizabeth's sixteenth birthday, she registered for war service, and two years later she became counsellor of state and signed her first act of Parliament. Shortly before the end of World War II, Elizabeth was trained to drive heavy transport vehicles and to repair them.

In the summer of 1947, Elizabeth announced her engagement to Prince Philip, her cousin and also a descendant from Queen Victoria. Elizabeth—with her Venus in Pisces—felt she had found her ideal mate. Her father, however, did everything in his power to dissuade Elizabeth from marrying Philip. In contrast, Lord Mountbatten, Philip's uncle, did everything in his power to promote this union despite the considerable number of obstacles to be overcome prior to marriage between Elizabeth and Philip. Philip had to become a British citizen and convert from his native Greek Orthodox religion to Anglican. As a member of the Greek royal family, Philip would have to adopt a surname and he chose Mountbatten at the suggestion of his uncle, Lord Mountbatten, who was Viceroy of India. Furthermore, Philip's financial assets amounted to all of 20 pounds and all his belongings fit into three suitcases. Philip's weekly salary in the British Royal Navy was a paltry eleven pounds per week. Undaunted by obstacles, Elizabeth forged ahead and the couple was married in Westminster Abbey on November 20, 1947 (progressed Midheaven trine Moon, ruler of her seventh house). The press went wild praising the tall, thin, blond groom who looked like a Viking god. The couple had been corresponding with each other for six years, and although this was an *arranged* union, they appeared to be genuinely in love with each other.

The first child of this marriage, Prince Charles, was born in November 1948 (Elizabeth's progressed Midheaven square Venus, progressed Ascendant conjunct Mars) and in August 1950 Princess Anne was born (progressed Ascendant conjunct Jupiter). Feeling that she had performed her duty to her country by providing two heirs, Elizabeth reportedly decided she and Philip would henceforth have separate bedrooms. When on holiday in Kenya in February 1952, Elizabeth and Philip learned of the death of George VI (progressed Midheaven sesquiquadrate Sun, progressed Ascendant square Saturn). Elizabeth's coronation in June 1953 was televised and viewed around the world by millions. Despite their largely separate lives, Elizabeth and Philip apparently did on occasion manage to be intimate as evidenced by the birth of Prince Andrew in February 1960 (progressed Ascendant trine Venus), but the birth of Prince Edward four years later in March 1964 came as a complete surprise (progressed Midheaven square Uranus; progressed Ascendant trine Saturn). Elizabeth's family was now complete and their happiness became the focus of her life. Her sister Margaret had settled down with Lord Snowdon four year earlier, averting the constitutional crisis which could have erupted had Margaret insisted on marrying Peter Townsend, a divorced man.

Princess Anne, the first of Elizabeth's children to marry, was united in November 1973 with Mark Phillips; the event brought renewed attention to the royal family. Soon thereafter, Margaret separated from Lord Snowdon and Elizabeth began to worry that she might have to sanction a divorce—a *fait accompli* by 1978 (progressed Ascendant inconjunct Saturn). Meanwhile, the queen felt it was time for her bachelor son Prince Charles to settle down and marry—not to mention providing an heir to the throne. After extensive interviews, a suitable bride was found in Diana Spencer. The couple was married in St. Paul's Cathedral on July 29, 1981 (progressed Midheaven sextile Venus opposite Pluto). One year later, the long awaited heir, Prince William, was born.

The summer of 1982 was, to say the least, embarrassing to Queen Elizabeth. An unemployed laborer, Michael Fagan, broke into the palace and ensconced himself in the queen's private quarters. It took quite some time before the intruder could be ejected and soon thereafter a review of the security system was undertaken. The tabloids had a field day with the sexual cavortings of Prince Andrew in 1983 with the queen trying unsuccessfully to squelch the press from telling all. Elizabeth also put her foot down when Prince Charles tried to attend a private mass with the Pope. It seems her children were rebelling against the strict and authoritarian guidelines laid down by their mother.

The marriage of Prince Andrew to Sarah Ferguson in July 1986 really gave the papers *carte blanche*. Fergie's ample physique was splashed across the front page as was the uninhibited affection Fergie and Andrew expressed for each other. During this same period, Prince Edward left the Royal Marines, causing his father to foam at the mouth. Then Princess Anne separated from her husband in 1989 just as rumors of Diana's battles with eating disorders began to surface (progressed Midheaven inconjunct Neptune, progressed Ascendant square Mars).

In 1992—the *annus horibilis*, according to Elizabeth—her family seemed to fall apart. Anne and Mark were formally divorced, Andrew and Fergie decided to go their separate ways, and Charles and Diana had put up a front long enough and exposed the sham of their arranged union (progressed Midheaven sextile Saturn, progressed Ascendant opposite Saturn). Transiting Pluto was crossing the queen's Midheaven, bringing up sludge the royal family would have preferred to keep under wraps. Transiting Uranus and Neptune were straddling the queen's natal Ascendant, and publication of Andrew Morton's book on the Princess of Wales did little for maintaining the reputation of the monarchy the queen had tried so hard to ensure over the years. There were photos of Fergie's business advisor sucking her toes. It is amazing the queen did not have a nervous breakdown! Ever since Elizabeth invited television crews into the royal enclave in the late 1960s, the press has taken more and more liberties—exposing the often ugly underbelly of the monarchy—an institution many British feel is no longer relevant to modern life.

Windsor Castle burned in December 1992—a symbolic representation of the state of the monarchy which would have to resurrect itself from the ashes if it were to survive. The British were incensed when the queen asked for donations to help in the castle's restoration—ironic, considering the queen is, personally, one of the wealthiest women in the world. There were also rumblings about the queen's not paying her fair share of taxes. Well, the queen is now a taxpayer, just like everyone else. Further, she has opened Buckingham Palace to tourists during the summer months to help defray the expenses of restoring Windsor Castle, and she got rid of the royal yacht Britannia because she could no longer afford to renovate it. The foregoing is testament to what Pluto crossing the Midheaven can do to one's reputation as it exposes one's dirty laundry. It should also be noted that Pluto has transited Elizabeth's Saturn, ruler of her natal Ascendant—transforming her outlook as well as her lifestyle.

In early February 2002, her sister, Princess Margaret, died after a stroke. Seven weeks later, her mother, Elizabeth the Queen Mother, passed away at age 101 (Midheaven trine Mercury semisquare Venus/Uranus).

Elizabeth is the personification of a Capricorn. Always conservative, dutiful and responsible, she values her reputation and that of her family above all other things. She has tried to shield and protect her offspring from the harsh realities of the outside world as demonstrated by Cancer on her Descendant; however, she is somewhat deficient in demonstrating her affection toward her children. Princess Anne has been quoted as saying, "My mother hasn't got a maternal instinct in her body." With her Moon in Leo, image is everything in Elizabeth's eyes. Always moral and upright, Elizabeth has tried to do what is best for her country. In the process, her family, despite her good intentions, has often gotten short shrift. Her strict and stern demeanor has no doubt been difficult on her children, for when she came to the throne, she was told by her father to uphold the honor of the monarchy above all else because it had been so seriously damaged by Edward VIII's indiscretions some years before.

Prince Philip, Duke of Edinburgh

Philip was born at Mon Repos on the island of Corfu, Greece on June 10, 1921 at 10:00 a.m. EET according to the biography by Denis Judd. His family, including four older sisters, was forced to flee their homeland when he was a year old (progressed Midheaven trine Jupiter). They settled eventually in great Britain, where Philip joined the Royal Navy during World War II. After six years of corresponding with Princess Elizabeth, his uncle (Lord Mountbatten)

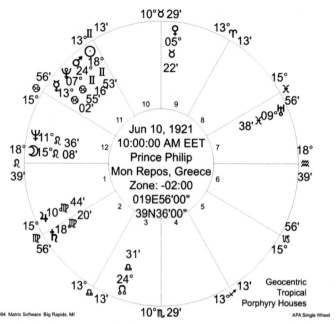

10°♉29'

13'♊13'

13°♊13'

☉18°

☿07°♊

♂24°♊

☾13°♊16'

♄56'

15°♋02'

♀05°♉22'

10   9

Jun 10, 1921
10:00:00 AM EET
Prince Philip
Mon Repos, Greece
Zone: -02:00
019E56'00"
39N36'00"

13°♈13'

15°♓56'

38'♓09°♓

18°♒39'

56'♑15°

13°♐13'

Geocentric
Tropical
Porphyry Houses

Ψ11°♌36'
♆15°♌08'

18°♌39'

11

12

1

8

7

6

5

2

3   4

♃10°♍44'
20'

18°♍

15°♍56'

♄

31'
♎24°♎

13°♎13'

10°♏29'

©1994 Matrix Software Big Rapids, MI

AFA Single Wheel

persuaded King George VI to let his daughter marry Philip. The couple was wed in November 1947 as Philip's progressed Ascendant opposed Uranus, ruler of his seventh house, which is also placed in the house of marriage. One year later, Prince Charles was born (progressed Ascendant conjunct Jupiter). After the birth of Princess Anne in August 1950 (progressed Midheaven square Uranus), the royal couple occupied separate bedrooms for nearly a decade. But, people change their minds—in February 1960 Prince Andrew was born (progressed Midheaven conjunct Sun) and four years later, Prince Edward came into the world (progressed Midheaven semisquare Venus).

With his Sun in verbal and witty Gemini, Philip has an opinion on nearly everything, often putting his foot in his mouth due to his blunt honesty. With the Sun conjunct Mars, Philip loves sports, especially anything having to do with horses, particularly polo. For a man with Leo rising, he has been described as being rather arrogant, selfish and demanding, often rude and overly aggressive. Philip has had to play third fiddle to his wife and son, Prince Charles, and this has not been an easy path for him to tread. Philip's jealousy of his son is legendary—to ask a Leo to walk behind those that British protocol dictates to be more important is contrary to the basic Leo nature. With the Moon rising above the Ascendant, Philip is seldom out of the limelight, although he often has to keep his more tender side under wraps and out of sight.

But Philip got back at the position he held in a typical Gemini fashion: He became a promiscuous man about town without the slightest feeling of guilt about betraying his marriage vows, according to a recent biography of the queen. Elizabeth often knew of her husband's indiscretions and simply looked the other way. It was not in her best interest to rein in her husband, especially as he had Uranus in the seventh house. So Philip went his own way with women like Alexandra of Kent, Queen Alexandra of Yugoslavia and several duchesses. Philip values appearance more than reality as shown by the Moon in Leo, for whom the show and the performance are everything. But remember, Elizabeth also has her Moon in Leo. The sin was not in doing those things, but in being caught. So much for royal prerogatives!

Philip is reputed to be a stern father due to the Sun squaring Saturn. Seldom affectionate toward his offspring, he keeps his distance due to Jupiter (ruler of the fifth house) opposite Uranus, which speaks to his need for freedom and elbow room Sometimes appearing self-righteous due to that rising Jupiter, Philip is continually restless and revels in long journeys overseas where he acts as an ambassador for the interests of Great Britain.

Charles, Prince of Wales

Charles Philip Arthur George, heir to the throne of Great Britain, Scotland, Northern Ireland and all overseas territories, future head of the commonwealth and possible future head of the Church of England, was born in Buckingham Palace on November 14, 1948 at 9:14 p.m. GMT, according to the *London Times.* His mother became queen when he was three years, three months old (progressed Midheaven opposing Venus). Charles was the first member of the royal family (with the exception of Edward VIII) to attend a public school (Gordunston), as shown by Mercury (ruler of the third house) semisquare Mars (ruler of his Midheaven).

Being a Scorpio with a rising Pluto makes Charles shy and secre-

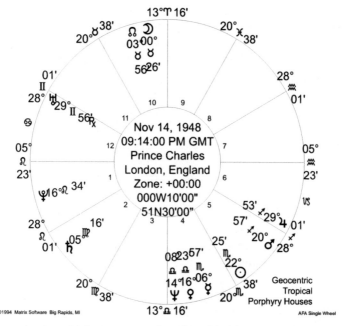

tive at times, which contrasts sharply with his Moon in the tenth
house, ensuring that he will seldom be out of the public eye. His
mother's influence is pervasive as is shown by the conjunction of
Charles' Moon to Elizabeth's Sun—almost to the minute. With Venus and Neptune conjunct in the fourth house, the Prince of Wales'
main interests are architecture, civic planning and urban renewal.
The Moon in Taurus gives him a penchant for gardening and a
strong sensitivity to growing things: He is said to talk to his plants,
much to the consternation and embarrassment of the royal family.
The rising Pluto also gives Charles an outspoken interest in medical
matters. He favors homeopathy like the rest of his family—something the royals do not wish to acknowledge in public.

But Venus and Neptune in the fourth house make Charles yearn
for the ideal domestic environment, something he thought he was
getting when he married Diana Spencer in July 1981 (progressed
Midheaven square Pluto inconjunct Venus). It was an arranged
match because, with Mars in the fifth house trine a rising Pluto,
Charles preferred the life of a bachelor—but history had dealt him a
different hand from the one he would have personally sought. It

was imperative that he marry and provide the country with an heir, so Charles reluctantly consented and, for a few years, the couple was happy. Following the initial rush of euphoria after the wedding, known in psychological circles as "limerence" or "infatuation," the spell soon wore off and the Prince and Princess of Wales went their separate ways—just as his parents had. Their personality traits and basic interests were vastly different. Charles loves to fish and play polo, while Diana preferred to dine at posh restaurants. Charles adores horses and being with nature; Diana reveled in discos and nightlife. Musically, Charles loves the classics, while Diana favored the Beatles and other pop artists. Charles reads philosophy and history, while Diana lost herself in romance novels. Charles seeks the company of intellectuals and Diana basked in the world of gossip and small talk. They obviously had little in common when they married and the gap grew wider with each passing year. Despite their Suns being trine, their Midheavens are opposite each other and their Moons are square by sign but not degree. Charles went back to his former mistress, Camilla Parker Bowles, who is descended from Alice Keppel, the last mistress to Edward VII.

Situations reached a boiling point for Charles and Diana in 1992 as his Midheaven was inconjunct Jupiter, ruler of the fifth house of love and romance. Charles' progressed Ascendant was in the process of conjuncting Saturn, not an indication of the happiest time of his life. True to his Scorpio nature, Charles retired to his country home, Highgrove, to tend his garden and find the solace demanded by those planets in his fourth house

Charles' horoscope promises glory and recognition, as well as resignation and isolation—not an easy dichotomy to balance. Being only a constitutional monarch will severely limit his political effectiveness, but whether his personality will be able to carry the weight his position demands should he become king is a matter yet to be seen. Rumors of his mother's stepping down have been rampant for years, but with Saturn conjunct Elizabeth's Midheaven and with Capricorn rising, if 1992 didn't make her hand in her resignation, nothing will cause her to step down. Charles will probably end up like his forebear King Edward VII and come to the throne late in life, possibly in his sixties.

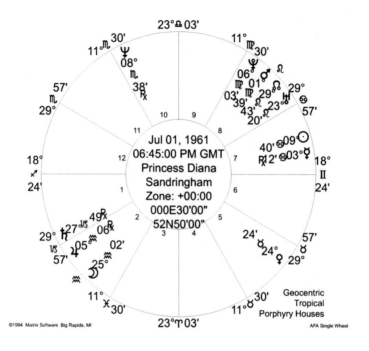

Geocentric
Tropical
Porphyry Houses

Charles and Diana finally were divorced in August 1996, after 15 years of marriage. One year later, on August 30, 1997, Diana was killed in an auto accident inside a tunnel near the Seine River in Paris (Midheaven sesquisquare Venus). In February 2002, his aunt, Princess Margaret, passed away and, one month later, his beloved grandmother, the Queen Mother Elizabeth, passed away (Midheaven inconjunct Mercury). It was a devastating loss for Charles, who had been extremely close to her. Finally, after a court-ship and love affair which lasted 34 years, Charles and his Mistress, Camilla Parker Bowles, tied the knot in April 2005 (Ascendant conjunct Venus/Pluto sesquisquare Moon) in a small but private ceremony at Windsor Castle.

Diana, Princess of Wales

According to palace sources, Diana Spencer was born at San-dringham, England on July 1, 1961 at 7:45 p.m. BST, according to her mother. Her parents divorced when she was young and, with Mars (ruler of her IC) conjunct Pluto in her eighth house, she no doubt carried a hidden resentment of the separation the rest of her life. Before she married the Prince of Wales, Diana taught school at a kindergarten in London. No doubt about it, Diana loved children and was a good mother to her two sons. Cancers need affection and need to be mothered as well as to nurture others.

Her marriage to Charles in July 1981 took place shortly after her Midheaven trined the Sun in her seventh house and the progressed Ascendant opposed Mercury, ruler of the Descendant. Transiting Pluto was sitting on her Midheaven and Neptune was also in aspect to her Midheaven, having crossed the Ascendant shortly before. The fact that the royal love affair did not work out as planned is shown by transiting Uranus on her wedding day filling out the T-square in her chart between the Moon, Venus and Uranus. By the time the royal couple filed for separation in December 1992, Diana's progressed Midheaven was squaring Uranus and opposing Venus.

Diana was divorced from Charles in August 1996. She was paid 17 million pounds as a settlement and was allowed to continue living in Kensington Palace. However, she was stripped of the title Her Royal Highness and would henceforth be known as Diana, Princess of Wales.

During the summer of 1997, Diana began seeing Dodi al-Fayed, son of Mohamed al-Fayed, owner of Harrod's department store and the Ritz Hotel in Paris. Speculation ran rife that Dodi was going to ask Diana to marry him as he had already been to a jeweler to pick out an engagement ring. But Dodi never got the chance as he and Diana were both killed during a high-speed car chase that caused their Mercedes to smash into a pole inside a tunnel along the river Seine in Paris. The date was August 30, 1997, and England erupted into an orgy of grief and sadness (Midheaven sextile Saturn, Ascendant sesquisquare Pluto in her eighth house of death).

The driver of the car was reputed to be drunk as he drove the car to excessive speeds to try to evade photographers who were chasing the car. The woman whom the British called their "Queen of Hearts" was brought home by her former husband, Charles. The televised funeral in Westminster Abbey was watched by millions around the world. Diana's brother delivered a diatribe against the royal family that sent tongues wagging, but Elton John stole the show when he sang a revised version of a song he wrote lauding

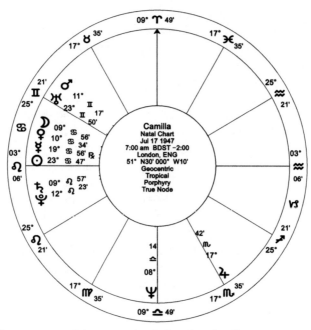

Camilla
Natal Chart
Jul 17 1947
7:00 am BDST −2:00
London, ENG
51° N30' 000° W10'
Geocentric
Tropical
Porphyry
True Node

Marilyn Monroe. Diana was buried on her family estate at Althorp on an island in the middle of a small lake.

Camilla Parker Bowles

Camilla was born in London on July 17, 1947 at 7:00 p.m. GDDT (5:00 a.m. GMT), according to *Camilla, the King's Mistress* by Caroline Graham. She first met Prince Charles at a polo match in the summer of 1971, whereby she reminded him that she was descended from Alice Keppel, a mistress to Edward VII, and asked Charles if he didn't want a go at it (Midheaven semisquare Mars/Uranus). The relationship cooled the following year when Charles went into the British Navy and Camilla decided to marry Andrew Parker Bowles in July 1973 (Midheaven sesquisquare Sun/Jupiter). She continued, however, to see Charles on the side until the Prince of Wales married Diana in July 1981 (Midheaven square Pluto, Ascendant semisquare Neptune sextile Uranus). Their affair resurfaced during the 1980s, causing considerable stress to the Princess of Wales, who called her "the Rottweiler." Charles and Diana separated in December 1992 (Midheaven sextile Sun sesquisquare Neptune), and in January 1995, Camilla divorced her husband (Midheaven semisquare Moon and Venus, Ascendant semisquare Mercury). Camilla laid low after Diana's death in August 1997, for obvious reasons. She was blamed by the British for being the cause of Charles' and Diana's breakup and was pelted with physical and verbal abuse. But by June 2000, Queen Elizabeth II said OK to Camilla's relationship with her son, and Camilla began to make public appearances with her lover and his two sons. She and Charles finally were married April 9, 2005 (Midheaven semisquare Mercury, Ascendant sextile Moon and Venus square Mars). Camilla will be known as Princess Consort, not Queen Camilla, when and if Charles ever ascends the throne.

Camilla is known to be bold and exuberant, with an earthy and bawdy sense of humor. She's warm and down-to-earth and enjoys having her own space. She and Charles have many things and interests in common, and her daredevil and rebellious streak really appeals to Charles. In many ways it's a pity that Charles didn't marry her back when he first met her as they're like two peas in a pod and really in love even after all these years. I wish them well.

Anne, the Princess Royal

Anne was born in Buckingham Palace on August 15, 1950 at 11:50 a.m. BST according to *The London Times*. As with her mother's chart, I believe Anne's reported birth time to be about ten to twelve minutes late. When her grandfather, King George VI, died, she was a year and a half old—her progressed Midheaven would have squared Mars in early 1952 if three degrees were subtracted from the reported birth time. The Midheaven would have been semisquare both Mercury and Saturn the following year when her mother was crowned. Anne married Mark Phillips in November 1973 when her progressed Midheaven would have been conjunct the Sun and the progressed Ascendant would have been trining Uranus—provided the slightly earlier birth time is used. Their son Peter Phillips was born in November 1977 and their daughter Zara Phillips was born in May 1981. The couple then began living apart and finally separated in 1989 (progressed Midheaven sextile Uranus, progressed Ascendant sextile Mercury-Saturn). Princess Anne and Mark Phillips were formally di-

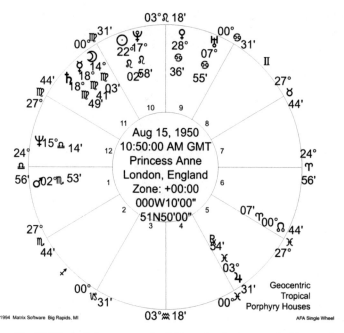

03°♌18'

00°♍31'

☿14° 18° 18° ♍ ♍ ☾ 49'

44' ♄ ♍ Ω03'
27°

☉ 22°♂17° Ψ
♌ Ω
02°58'

♀ 28°
♋
36'

♅07°
♋
55'

00° ♋31'

Ⅱ

27°
♉
44'

♓15°♎14'

24°
♎
56' ♂02°♏53'

10

11

12

9

8

Aug 15, 1950
10:50:00 AM GMT
Princess Anne
London, England
Zone: +00:00
000W10'00"
51N50'00"

1

2

3

7

6

5

4

24°
♈
56'

07'♈00°Ω44'

27°
♏
44'

♏ 00° ♑31'

R
54'
♓
03°
♃

27°
♓

00°♓31'

Geocentric
Tropical
Porphyry Houses

03°♒18'

©1994 Matrix Software Big Rapids, MI

AFA Single Wheel

vorced in 1992, and Anne married Timothy Laurence in December 1992, as her progressed Ascendant was applying to a square to her natal Sun.

Anne's arrogance and demanding nature were quite well known in her youth; however, she has matured into an honest and down to earth woman. Note the righteous Sun in Leo and rising Mars for confirmation of her aggressive spirit. Quite fond of horses, she became a royal equestrienne during the 1976 Olympics.

Despite being born under the royal sign, Anne has refused titles for her two children. Anne lives in an apartment near Kensington Palace where her expenses are taken care of by her mother since Anne was written off the Civil List.

Prince Andrew, Duke of York

Andrew was born February 19, 1960 at 3:30 p.m. GMT, according to *The London Times*. Educated for a career in the military due to Mars (ruler of the Midheaven) sitting in the sixth house of armed forces, Andrew attained fame and glory during the brief Falklands War of 1982 as his progressed Midheaven trined Saturn, ruler of his

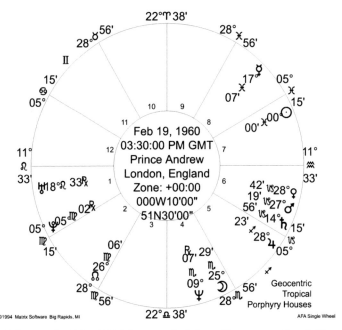

22°♈38'

28°♉56'

28°♓56'

Ⅱ

15'
♋
05°

17°☿
07'♓

05°
♓
15'

10   9

11

00'♐00°☉

Feb 19, 1960
03:30:00 PM GMT
Prince Andrew
London, England
Zone: +00:00
000W10'00"
51N30'00"

12

8

7

11°
♌
33'

11°
♒
33'

1

♅18°♌33♀

02♀♍

6

42'♑28°♀
19'♑
56'♑27°♂
23'♐14°♄15'

05°♀♍05°
♍
15'

2

5

06'
♍
26°
♎
28°
♍56'

3   4

07'29°♏
♏
09°25°
♏
☽56'
28°♏

♐
28°
4♑
05°

Geocentric
Tropical
Porphyry Houses

22°♎38'

©1994 Matrix Software Big Rapids, MI

AFA Single Wheel

sixth house. In July 1986, he married the effervescent Sarah Ferguson as his Midheaven squared Uranus (ruler of the Descendant) and his Ascendant had progressed to a trine of Jupiter. The difficulties in their marriage were also shown by the progressed Ascendant inconjunct Venus, ruler of his fourth house of security and home life. Despite being called a brash and vulgar woman at times, Fergie brought a breath of fresh air into the stuffy world of the royals. Her weight problem caused the press to dub her the Duchess of Pork as a parody on her royal title, the Duchess of York. Her indiscretions with her reputed business advisor provided the straw that broke the camel's back. Andrew was incensed and filed for separation in 1992, as his Midheaven opposed the Moon. Andrew and Fergie were formally divorced in April 1996 (Midheaven square Sun sesquisquare Saturn, Ascendant sesquisquare Venus/Saturn.

Andrew's past is nothing to brag about—except for scandal mongers. Once known as Randy Andy, his romps with women of dubious distinction, such as a soft porn actress, no doubt caused the queen to recoil in horror. Note that Andrew's Venus-Mars conjunction sextiles the sexy Moon in Scorpio. Despite his frequent

185

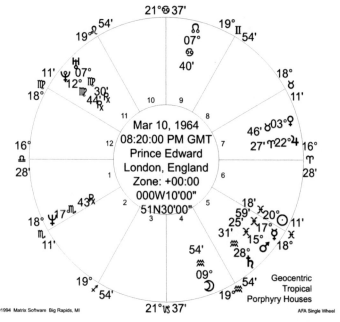

21°♋37'

19°♌54'

♌ 07° ♋ 40'

19°♊54'

11' ♅ 07° ♍

12° ♍

♍ 30' 44'℞ ℞

18°♏

18°♉11'

10   9

46' ♉03°♀

27' ♈22°♃   16°♈28'

16°♎28'

11   8

Mar 10, 1964
08:20:00 PM GMT
Prince Edward
London, England
Zone: +00:00
000W10'00"
51N30'00"

12

7

1

6

43'℞

2

5

18° ♏

3   4

18' 59' ♓20°

25' ♓17°☉ 11'

31' ♓15°☿

28' ♒ ♂ 18°

♓

18° ♏

18° ♏

17° ♏

11'

54'

♒ 09° ☽

19°♒54'

19° ♐54'

Geocentric
Tropical
Porphyry Houses

21°♑37'

©1994 Matrix Software Big Rapids, MI

AFA Single Wheel

brushes with scandal, Andrew is said to be the queen's favorite child. With Leo rising he is a romantic at heart; recently Andrew and Fergie have begun seeing each other again, so they may one day patch up their differences. Like his brother Prince Charles, Andrew has Neptune in the fourth house, causing him to yearn for a quiet and serene domestic life, which being a royal seldom guarantees.

Prince Edward

The youngest child of Elizabeth and Philip was born on March 10, 1964 in London at 8:20 p.m. GMT according to *The London Times*. Being so far down the list to inherit the throne has no doubt given Edward considerable latitude to do his own thing. To please his father, Edward joined the Royal Marines, but after a few weeks he quit, severely irritating and disappointing Philip. Edward preferred to spend time with theater people and in acting out roles on the stage. Rumors once flew about that he might be gay. Edward married Sophie Rhys-Jones, a public relations executive, in June 1999 (Midheaven conjunct Sun). He and his wife assumed the title

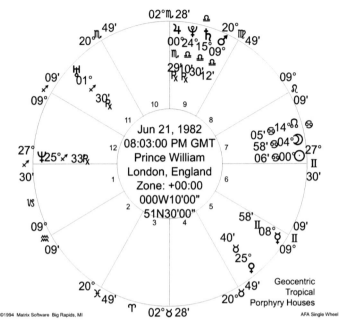

Chart labels:

02°♏28' ♎

20°♏49'

4 ♆ ♄ ♂
00°24°15°09°
♏ ♎ ♎ ♎
29°10°30°12'
Rx Rx

20° ♍49'

09° ♐
♅ 01°
09° ♐ 30'Rx

09° ♌
09°

Jun 21, 1982
08:03:00 PM GMT
Prince William
London, England
Zone: +00:00
000W10'00"
51N30'00"

10   9

11   8

12   7

1

2   5

3   4

6

05' ⊛14°♌ ⊛
58' ⊛04°☽
06' ⊛00°☉ 27°
♊

27° ♐
♓25°♐33Rx
30'

♑

09° ♒
09'

58'
♊08° ☿ ♊
40'
♂
25° ♊ 09°
♀

20°
♓49'

Geocentric
Tropical
20°♉49' Porphyry Houses

♈ 02°♉28'

©1994 Matrix Software Big Rapids, MI

AFA Single Wheel

of Early and Countess of Wessex. A daughter was born to them November 8, 2003 (Ascendant sextile Pluto).

Prince William

William was born in a hospital in Paddington, a borough of London, on June 21, 1982 at 9:03 p.m. BST according to *The London Times.* Like his mother, William has Sun in Cancer with Sagittarius rising. His angles are similar to those of both Elizabeth I and Edward VII, so when he comes to the throne a glorious age may begin for Great Britain. Ironically, the progressed angles were not affected during the year his parents formally separated. When his parents' divorce was finalized in August 1996, William's progressed Ascendant was sesquisquare natal Venus. One year later, on August 30, 1997, when his mother was killed in a car crash, William's progressed Midheaven was sesquisquare his Sun/Moon midpoint and the Ascendant squared the natal Mars/Saturn midpoint. Since his mother's death, William has become much closer to his father and his approval of Charles' relationship with Camilla enabled his father to finally marry her.

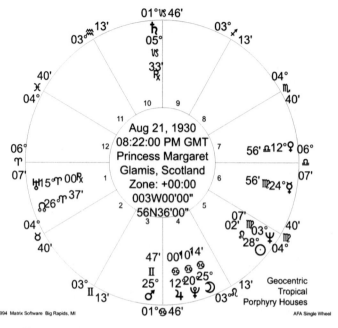

01°♑46'

03°♒13'

♄
05°
♑
33'
℞

03°♐13'

40'
♓
04°

04°
♏
40'

10   9

11   8

Aug 21, 1930
08:22:00 PM GMT
Princess Margaret
Glamis, Scotland
Zone: +00:00
003W00'00"
56N36'00"

06°
♈
07'

12   7

56' ♎12°♀ 06°
♎

♅15°♈00'℞

1   6

56' ♍24°☿ 07'

☊26°♈37'

2   5

3   4

04°
♉
40'

07'
02' ♍03°♀ 40'
☽28°☉ ♍
04°

47' 00'0'4'
♊
25°
☌

♋ ♋ ♋
12°20°25°
♃ ♆ ☽

Geocentric
Tropical
Porphyry Houses

03°
♊13'

13'

03°♌

01°♋46'

©1994 Matrix Software Big Rapids, MI

AFA Single Wheel

Princess Margaret

Margaret was born at Glamis Castle in Scotland on August 21, 1930 at 9:22 p.m. BST according to *The London Times*. Her uncle Edward VIII abdicated when she was six, making her father, George VI, the king (progressed Ascendant square Moon sextile Mars). Fifteen years later, in early 1952, her father died, making her sister Elizabeth Queen of England (progressed Midheaven opposing Moon). Soon thereafter, Margaret began dating Peter Townsend, a divorced man. Her sister initially tried to remain aloof, but finally stepped in to remind Margaret of her responsibility to her position. Margaret gave up the man she loved in late 1955 (progressed Midheaven inconjunct Mars, progressed Ascendant square Neptune).

Four years later, in early 1960, Margaret married Anthony Armstrong Jones, a society photographer whom she had met on the club circuit (progressed Ascendant trine Venus, ruler of Descendant in the seventh house). The couple had two children: David, the Viscount Linley, born in November 1961, and Lady Sarah Chatto, born in May 1964. Margaret's husband was given the title of Lord Snowdon. Over the years, Margaret and Tony began to go their separate ways. Loving the jet set life, Margaret caused quite a scandal in the mid-1970s when she was found vacationing on Mustique in the Caribbean on the arm of a much younger man. Not too long thereafter, Margaret filed for divorce much to the dismay of the queen, and by 1978 became the first royal to be granted a divorce since Henry VIII (progressed Midheaven semisquare Saturn inconjunct Pluto). Margaret is often seen around London in posh clubs, smoking cigarettes (she is the only member of the royal family who openly smokes) and sometimes drinking a bit too much.

Margaret had been in declining health during her sixties. She died of a stroke on February 9, 2002, only seven weeks before her mother passed away (Midheaven trine Jupiter sesquisquare Moon, Ascendant semisquare Neptune).

Margaret has a difficult chart. The wide cardinal cross on the angles does not promise an easy or happy life. Note that Venus in the seventh house and ruler of the Descendant squares Jupiter, ruler of the ninth house, indicative of her family's disapproval of her affair with Townsend. Venus also opposes Uranus—a strong indication of separation or divorce down the road. Margaret's Sun in Leo in the fifth house shows her love of the café and theater crowd and her reputation for being quite a jet setter. With Saturn at the Midheaven, her options from birth were rather limited due to matters of protocol, but Uranus rising made her be true to herself—come hell or high water. Margaret was the black sheep of the royal family until recently when her nieces's and nephews' cavorting made her earlier flings seem like kid stuff.

Queen Mother Elizabeth

I saved the best for last. Elizabeth Bowes Lyon, most popular of the royals and daughter of the fourteenth Earl of Strathmore, was born August 4, 1900. That is the only fact about which all sources are in agreement. Her birthplace is given as both London and St. Paul's Waldenbury, which is the ancestral home of the Strathmores. Her birth time has been given as either shortly after midnight or close to noon. I use 11:31 a.m. (as noted in Sabian Symbols by Marc E. Jones) but prefer the locale of London as her

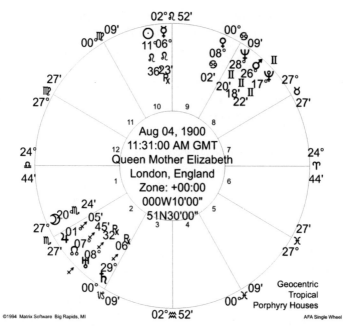

02°♌52'

00♍09'

00♍09'

27' ♍ 27°

24° ♎ 44'

27°♏ 27'

00° ♑ 09'

02°♒52'

00° ♈ 09'

00° ♋ 09'

02° ♊ 27° ♉ 27'

24° ♈ 44'

27' ♓ 27°

00° ♑ 09'

⊙ ☿ 11°06'
♌ ♌
36°23' ℞

♀ 08° ⊛
⊛ 02'
♆ 28°
20' ♊ 26 ♂ ♊
18' ♊ 17 ♅
22'

20° ♏ 24' 05'
01° 45'℞
07° 32'℞
08° 06'
☊ 08° ♄ 29°

Aug 04, 1900
11:31:00 AM GMT
Queen Mother Elizabeth
London, England
Zone: +00:00
000W10'00"
51N30'00"

Geocentric
Tropical
Porphyry Houses

©1994 Matrix Software Big Rapids, MI

AFA Single Wheel

mother was on vacation at the time.

Queen Mother Elizabeth married Albert, Duke of York and second son of King George V and Queen Mary, on April 27, 1923 in Westminster Abbey (progressed Midheaven sextile Mars, ruler of the Descendant; progressed Ascendant square Sun, ruler of the Midheaven). Three years later Princess Elizabeth was born (progressed Midheaven sextile Neptune, ruler of the fifth house) and in the summer of 1930, Princess Margaret came into the world (progressed Midheaven square Jupiter). As King Edward VIII's affair with Wallis Simpson intensified during the early 1930s, Elizabeth seriously wondered whether the prediction made by a gypsy when she was a young woman would come true. The gypsy had told her that one day she would be queen—a fact that had seemed way off the mark at the time. But when Edward VIII abdicated the throne in December 1936, making her husband King of England, the prediction came to pass (progressed Midheaven sextile Venus, ruler of the Ascendant; progressed Ascendant conjunct the Moon).

Three years later, as war raged on the continent of Europe, Hitler began bombing the East End of London. Rather than escape to the country, the royal family decided to tough it out in Buckingham Palace to show the British, not to mention the Germans, the resilience and stubborn persistence of the English. It was an act that permanently endeared George and Elizabeth in the hearts of their countrymen and elevated the monarchy to great heights. But the war took its toll on George's health, a condition which Elizabeth blamed on Wallis Simpson and for which she never forgave her. George VI died of cancer in February 1952 at age fifty-six (progressed Ascendant inconjunct Neptune).

Libra rising gives the Queen Mother a tactful, charming and polite disposition and demeanor—always with a kind word for everyone, seldom provoking or bending to controversy. Her serene manner and ever present smile radiate from the depths of her being—characteristic of the prominent Sun in Leo at the top of her chart. She seems to look good, regardless of what she wears, and is seldom seen without one of her famous hats. With Libra rising, she prefers loose fitting and flowing gowns and dresses, always tasteful and fashionable, never gaudy. Her Moon in Scorpio gave her the strength, endurance and tenacity to stick it out during the darker hours of the war; it also made the royal couple a model for their subjects to follow. Elizabeth's husband George had Moon in Scorpio in addition to his natal Ascendant and Midheaven being in the same sign and very close by to Elizabeth's Ascendant and Midheaven. Elizabeth's Venus in Cancer shows her to have been very maternal and a good mother to her two daughters, but it also points to her being the mother of England and a figurehead to emulate and adore. The planets in her eighth house have no doubt had a great deal to do with her longevity—she outlived her husband by more than five decades.

In February 2002, her youngest daughter, Princess Margaret, passed away after a stroke. On March 30, 2002, the beloved Queen Mother died at the age of 101 (Midheaven square Sun sesquisquare Mars, Ascendant semisquare Moon inconjunct Mercury).

Bibliography

Monarch	Book	Author
William I	*William the Conqueror*	David Douglas
Henry II	*Henry Plantagenet*	Richard Barber
Eleanor of Aquitaine	*Eleanor of Aquitaine and the Four Kings*	Amy Kelly
Richard I	*Richard, Coeur de Lion*	Philip Henderson
John	*Maligned Monarch*	Alan Lloyd
Henry III	*Henry III and Lord Edward*	Frederick Powicke
Edward I	*Edward I*	L.F. Salzman
Edward II	*Edward II*	Harold Hutchinson
Edward III	*Edward III and the Scots*	Ronald Nicolson
Richard II	*The Hollow Crown*	Harold Hutchinson
Henry IV	*Henry IV of England*	J.L. Kirby
Henry V	*King Henry V*	Harold Hutchinson
Henry VI	*King Rene D'Anjou*	S. Edgecumbe
Edward IV	*The Sun of York*	Mary Clive
Richard III	*Richard III*	Paul Kendall
Henry VII	*Henry VII*	S.B. Chrimes
Henry VIII	*Henry VIII*	Lacey Smith
Edward VI	*The Last Tudor King*	Hester Chapman
Mary I	*The Lady Mary*	Milton Waldman
Elizabeth I	*Elizabeth the Great*	Elizabeth Jenkins
James I	*James the Sixth and First*	David Wilson
Charles I	*Charles I*	Christopher Hibbert
Charles II	*Charles II*	Antonia Fraser
Mary II	*William's Mary*	Elizabeth Hamilton
William III	*William of Orange*	Nesca Robb
Anne	*Queen Anne*	David Green
George I	*George I*	Henry Imbert
Geroge III	*The King Who Lost America*	Alan Lloyd
George IV	*George IV*	Roger Fulford
William IV	*King William IV*	Philip Ziegler
Victoria	*Queen Victoria*	Elizabeth Longford
Edward VII	*King Edward VII*	Philip Magnus
George V	*King George V*	Harold Nicolson
Edward VIII	*A King's Story*	Duke of Windsor
George VI	*King George VI*	John Wheeler-Bennett
Elizabeth II	*Undoubted Queen*	H.T. Miller

General Biographies

Kings and Queens of England   Eric Delderfield
Lives of the Kings and   Antonia Fraser
   Queens of England
Crown of A Thousand Years   M.E. Hudson
Queens of England   Norah Lofts
Chronicle of the Royal Family   Derrik Mercer
Oxford Illustrated History
   of England   Kenneth Morgan
Kings and Queens of England   Jane Murray

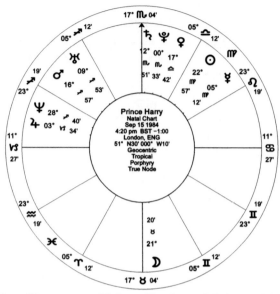

Prince Harry, son of Prince Charles and Princess Diana.
Source: *London Times*

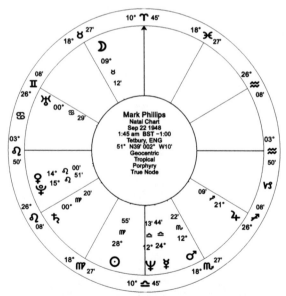

Mark Phillips, first husband of Princess Anne.
Source: doctor said between 1:30 and 2:00 a.m.

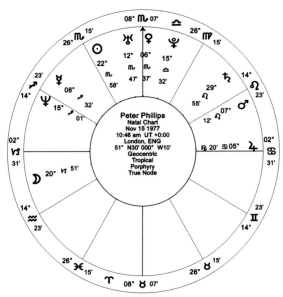

Peter Phillips, son of Princess Anne and Mark Phillips.
Source: *London Times*

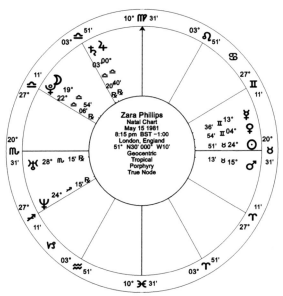

Zara Phillips, daughter of Princess Anne and Mark Phillips.
Source: *London Times*

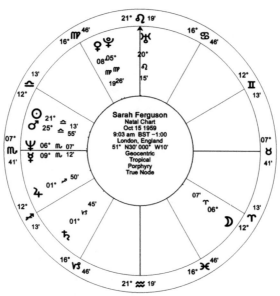

Sarah Ferguson, Duchess of York and wife of Prince Andrew.
Source: Buckingham Palace

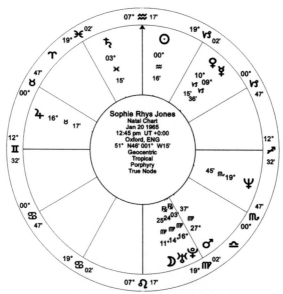

Sophie Rhys Jones, wife of Prince Edward.
Lois Rodden quotes Erin Sullivan for between 12:30 and 1:00 p.m.

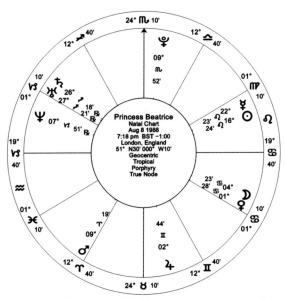

Princess Beatrice, daughter of Prince Andrew and Sarah Ferguson.
Source: *London Times*

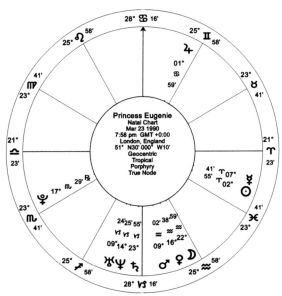

Princess Eugenie, daughter of Prince Andrew and Sarah Ferguson.
Source: *London Times*

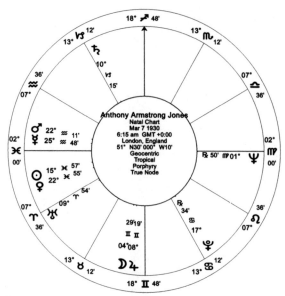

Anthony Armstrong Jones, husband of Princess Margaret.
Source: from him to astrologer, Marion Meyer Drew

Timothy Lawrence,
second husband of Princess Anne.
March 1, 1955, England; time and city unavailable.

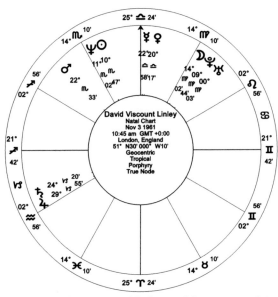

David Viscount Linley, son of Princess Margaret and Anthony Armstrong Jones. Source: *London Times*

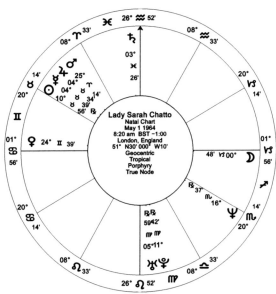

Lady Sarah Chatto, daughter of Princess Margaret and Anthony Armstrong Jones. Source: *London Times*

Printed in the United States
200132BV00002B/313-330/A

9 780866 904537